Air Fryer Cookbook

Best 100+ Healthy, Delicious and Easy Recipes for Your Family

Written by: Jolene Daisy

Copyright © 2017

All rights reserved.

All rights Reserved. No part of this publication or the information in it may be quoted from or reproduced in any form by means such as printing, scanning, photocopying or otherwise without prior written permission of the copyright holder.

Disclaimer and Terms of Use:

Effort has been made to ensure that the information in this book is accurate and complete, however, the author and the publisher do not warrant the accuracy of the information, text and graphics contained within the book due to the rapidly changing nature of science, research, known and unknown facts and internet. The Author and the publisher do not hold any responsibility for errors, omissions or contrary interpretation of the subject matter herein. This book is presented solely for motivational and informational purposes only.

Dedication

I dedicate this book to my family.

Table of Contents

INTRODUCTION 6
- Is it Possible to Fry without Oil? 6
- How Does an Air Fryer Work? 6
- The Requirements for Healthier Cooking 7
- Others Benefits of Using Air Fryers 7
- This cookbook is your trusty Air Fryer guide 8

AIR FRYER BREAKFAST RECIPES 9
- Cheese & Basil Omelet 9
- Cinnamon Toast 10
- Avocado and Greek Yogurt on Sourdough 11
- Breakfast Potatoes 12
- Potato Pancakes 13
- Spinach & Feta Frittata 14
- Strawberry Cream Cheese Toasts 15
- Breakfast Bagel Sandwich 16
- Banana Bread 17
- Breakfast Sausages 18
- Fried Baked Eggs 19

AIR FRYER VEGETABLES & SIDE DISHES RECIPES 20
- Sweet Potato Chips 20
- Baked Baby Potatoes 21
- Roasted Brussel Sprouts and Butternut Squash 22
- French Fries 23
- Zucchini Ricotta Puffs 24
- Crispy Sesame Tofu Bites 25
- Eggplant Chips 26
- Roasted Florets 27
- Baked Corn 28
- Taro Batonnet 29
- Crispy Onion Rings 30

AIR FRYER CHICKEN RECIPES 31
- Lemon & Garlic Chicken 31
- Air Fried Chicken Wings 32
- Rosemary Chicken Drumsticks 33
- Lemon Parmesan Chicken Wings 34
- Honey Sriracha Wings 35
- Chicken Spring Roll 36
- Guilt-Free BBQ Wings 37
- Baked Lemon Chicken Fillet 38
- Honey Butter Wings 39
- Paprika & Pepper Sauce Wings 40
- Lime Chili Chicken 41
- Herbed Chicken Tenders 42
- Roasted Rosemary Chicken Thighs 43
- Chicken Burrito 44

- Marinated Chicken Kebabs 45
- Chicken & Spinach Samosa with Cucumber Raita 46
- Air-fry Roasted Chicken 48
- Tex-Mex Wings with Blue Cheese Dip 49

AIR FRYER BEEF & PORK RECIPES 50

- Roasted Boneless Pork Chop 50
- Garlic Beef Steak 51
- Easy Pork Ribs 52
- Classic Sirloin Steak Recipe 53
- Air Fried Beef Patties 54
- Pork Tenderloin 55
- Sweet & Sour Pork 56
- Beef Meatballs 57
- Pork in Yogurt Bites 58
- Homemade Meatloaf 59
- Air Stir Fry Beef with Carrots and Spinach 60
- Beef with Pepper and Mushrooms 61
- Grilled Pork Chop and Kale Chips 62
- Pork Ribs 63
- Beef Goulash 64
- Pork Schnitzel in Mushroom Sauce 65
- Minced Pork with Fresh Coriander 66
- Air Fried Pork with Ketchup 67

AIR FRYER FISH & SEAFOOD RECIPES 68

- Spicy Coconut Macadamia Catfish 68
- Quick & Easy Crispy Lemon Cod 69
- Corn Flakes Crusted White Swai 70
- Light Beer-Battered Fish & Chips 71
- Parmesan-Crusted Tilapia Fillet 72
- Roasted Prawns 73
- Crispy Breaded Shrimps 74
- Salmon Steak 75
- Fried Calamari Rings 76
- Trout Fillet 77
- Tuna Steak 78
- Air Fried Dover Sole 79
- Grilled Lemon Soy Halibut 80
- Fish Pie 81
- Baked Scallops 82
- Salmon in Teriyaki Steak Sauce 83

AIR FRYER VEGETARIAN RECIPES 84

- Air Fried Asparagus 84
- Tomato and Olive in Phyllo Pastry 85
- Vegetarian Paella 86
- Stewed Tomato Soup 87
- Roasted Curry Vegetables 88
- Vegetarian Sandwich 89

Vegetarian Noodle Soup ... 90
Eggplant Parmigiana ... 91
Tofu with Broccoli ... 92
Oyster Mushrooms ... 93
Veggie Spring Rolls ... 94
Veggie Balls ... 95
Healthy Vegetarian Casserole ... 96
Vegetable Ragout ... 97
Vegetarian Quesadilla ... 98
Baked Stuffed Mushrooms ... 99
Air Fried Chickpeas ... 100

AIR FRYER BAKING & DESSERTS RECIPES ... 101

Carrot Cake ... 101
Donut recipe ... 102
Orange Cupcakes ... 103
Blueberry Muffins ... 104
Chocolate Brownie ... 105
Scones ... 106
Oatmeal Cookies ... 107
Cornbread Muffin ... 108
The Healthy Pound Cake ... 109
Vanilla Tart ... 110
New York Cheesecake ... 111

CONCLUSION ... 112

Introduction

Is it Possible to Fry without Oil?

Frying is a cooking method that involves food in contact with hot fat, such as oil. Both the temperature of the fat and cooking time affect the texture and taste of the fried food.

Traditionally, a frying pan or a deep-fryer is used by home cooks and even cooking professionals. For many years, they're the standard tools to fry items such as eggs, fish, poultry, vegetables, pork, beef, and even some pastries.

A significant innovation in home cooking happened when electronics company Philips invented a kitchen appliance called air fryer. Their AirFryer was launched in 2013 at the IFA consumer electronics show in Berlin and positioned as an alternative to traditional frying.

Since then, other companies have followed suit and produced their own air cookers.

How Does an Air Fryer Work?

The concept of an air fryer is to fry food items in the air instead of oil. This revolutionary kitchen appliance uses superheated air that circulates to cook the food. This way, you don't have to dunk your food in sizzling hot fat just to achieve that crunch.

Philips' used the patented Rapid Air Technology (fast and precise circulating hot air) to develop its AirFryer. It uses a grill and fan to circulate extremely hot air (up to 200 degrees Celsius), achieving that browning and crisping process quite well. This is known as the Maillard effect.

Based on conducted cooking tests, Philips claims its air fryers can cut down fat usage by up to 80%.

Regarding structure, an air fryer almost looks like a large rice cooker but with a front door handle. It has a removable chunky tray that holds the food to the air fried. It has an integrated timer to allow you to pre-set cooking times, and an adjustable temperature control so you can pre-set the best cooking temperature.

Different models offer different features, such as digital displays, auto-power shut-off, but mostly they work the same and use the same technology.

The Requirements for Healthier Cooking

With the growing demand for healthier cooking and better nutrition, people have turned to the air fryer as an alternative way of cooking without fat. After all, too much fat from fried foods in one's diet contributes to obesity and cardiovascular diseases.

However, fat really does make food palatable. No wonder it's tough to give up that pleasant fried taste.

With an air fryer, though, you capture the great taste of fried foods without the use of oil. It's a practical way for anyone striving to become slim and healthy.

Others Benefits of Using Air Fryers

It's versatile and multi-functional.

Despite its name, air fryers not only fry food, but also roast, bake, and grill. With the right accessories, it can perform cooking methods beyond mere frying. Its *versatility* makes it a handy appliance to add to your kitchen arsenal.

Some models may allow you to cook different items without them being together simultaneously. That way, the taste and odor of on are not transferred to the other.

It has a compact design.

Air fryers vary in cooking capacity, with some models able to cook up to 1.2 kg. This is the perfect size for a family of 5. But no matter how big its capacity it, the air fryer's design and compact size is *suitable even for small kitchens.*

It cuts down cooking time and calories.

According to Philips guidelines, a batch of homemade chips needs just half a tablespoonful of oil and will take 12 minutes to cook. Oven-ready French fries crisp even faster at 9 minutes. That's a lot of difference in time and oil compared to traditional deep-frying.

It's safer than traditional frying.

The air fryer is usually safer than traditional frying as there are no hot liquids that could splatter around. If you fry using chip pan over open flames, the risk of fire is high.

It's comfortable to maintain and clean.

The components of an air fryer are non-stick and dishwasher-safe. With regular cleaning and proper use, the air fryer can help lessen the frequency of heavy cleaning. You may not even have to do the usual scrubbing of frying pans and roasting trays anymore.

Plus, air fryers usually have an air filter to help control odor in the kitchen. Cooking becomes a pleasant experience as you won't have to bear that fried food smell all over.

With all these features and benefits, the air fryer is indeed a breakthrough in healthy home cooking. Who could ask for anything more?

This cookbook is your trusty Air Fryer guide

This cookbook offers you 101 air fryer recipes that are quick, tasty and healthy. You'll find a range recipe from breakfast items to chicken, fish, seafood, pork, beef, vegetables, side dishes, vegetarian, baked items and desserts.

Each recipe showcases the nutritional content so you can adapt the meals according to your preferred diet.

I hope that in this cookbook you'll find the best air fryer recipe for your needs.

Air Fryer Breakfast Recipes

Cheese & Basil Omelet

Prep time: 5 min | **Cooking time**: 10 min | **Servings** 4

What's breakfast without an omelet? This traditional breakfast staple takes a spin as it combines the familiar taste of cheddar cheese with the freshness of basil leaves.

Cheddar cheese is a good source of calcium, so adding this to your omelet will contribute to your daily calcium needs.

To make this omelet even healthier, use only the egg whites. For this recipe, though, we'll use whole eggs to give you enough protein to boost your day. It's really your choice.

Ingredients:

- 4 eggs
- ½ cup cheddar, grated
- 1 onion, diced
- ¼ cup basil leaves, shredded
- ¼ teaspoon salt
- ⅛ teaspoon black pepper

Directions:

1. Pre-heat the air fryer to 350 F.
2. In a bowl, beat the eggs together until well aerated. Add the cheese, onion and basil leaves and blend. Season with salt and black pepper.
3. Pour the beaten egg mixture into the baking accessory of your air fryer, or onto a baking pan that will fit your basket.
4. Cook for 10 minutes.
5. Transfer to a serving dish, and enjoy..

Nutritional Info (per serving):

- ✓ Calories – 99
- ✓ Fat – 5.4 g
- ✓ Fiber – 0.6 g
- ✓ Carbs – 3.3 g
- ✓ Protein – 9.3 g
- ✓ Sodium – 297 mg

Cinnamon Toast

Prep time: 5 min | **Cooking time**: 5 min | **Servings** 8

Cinnamon Toast perfectly complements a cup of hot cappuccino and will cheer you up.

Ingredients:

- 8 Slices of bread
- ½ a cup of sugar
- 1 stick of salted butter
- 1 ½ teaspoons of ground cinnamon
- 1 ½ teaspoons of vanilla extract
- Fresh ground black pepper to taste

Directions:

1. Mashup your soft butter using a fork.
2. Add the pepper, sugar, cinnamon, vanilla to the butter. Stir the whole mixture and combine well.
3. Spread the mixture on top of your bread, making sure to cover the entire surface.
4. Prepare as many slices as you want and place them in the Air Fryer Basket.
5. Cook them for about 5 minutes at 400°Fahrenheit (205°C).
6. Remove the bread slices from the fryer and serve hot!

Nutritional Info (per serving):

- ✓ Calories – 176
- ✓ Fat – 11.8 g
- ✓ Fiber – 0.5 g
- ✓ Carbs – 17.5 g
- ✓ Protein – 0.8 g
- ✓ Sodium – 143 mg

Avocado and Greek Yogurt on Sourdough

Prep time: 5 min | **Cooking time**: 5 min | **Servings** 4

When you need a power breakfast to start your day, this recipe is your best ally. With super food avocado in the spotlight, you can be sure this open-faced sandwich will give you the nutritional punch where you need it.

Avocados give you a mouthfeel so smooth and creamy you may forget it packs tons of nutrients. It's rich in potassium and vitamin E, antioxidants, and naturally low in salt. Mainly, it's composed of monounsaturated fat, which is one of the healthiest fats out there.

So go ahead and try this recipe. It's heart-friendly, and palate-friendly too.

Ingredients:

- 4 slices sourdough bread
- 1 whole avocado, sliced
- 2 tomatoes, sliced
- ½ lemon (juice)
- 200 g plain Greek yogurt
- 1 tablespoon honey
- ⅛ teaspoon sea salt
- ⅛ teaspoon black pepper
- alfalfa sprouts (optional)

Directions:

1. Pre-heat the air fryer to 400 F.
2. Slice the avocado and tomatoes into about ¼ inch thick slices. Squeeze half a lemon on the avocados to avoid discoloration. Set aside.
3. Place the sourdough bread slices in the air fryer and toast for 5 minutes or until golden brown and crunchy.
4. Spread Greek yogurt on each of the toasted bread, and drizzle with honey. Season with salt and pepper.
5. Lay the avocado slices over the Greek yogurt spread.
6. Top the avocado slices with tomatoes.
7. You may also garnish with alfalfa sprouts, but this is optional.
8. Serve.

Nutritional Info (per serving):

- ✓ Calories – 159
- ✓ Fat – 1.7 g
- ✓ Fiber – 1.8 g
- ✓ Carbs – 27.5 g
- ✓ Protein – 9.4 g
- ✓ Sodium – 243 mg

Breakfast Potatoes

Prep time: 5 min | **Cooking time**: 20 min | **Servings** 4

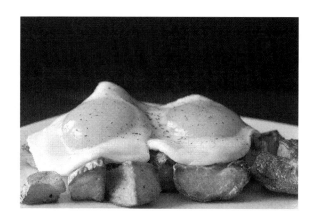

Aside from eggs, potatoes are popular mainstays on anyone's breakfast table. Well, we can't blame those who love potatoes. They're starchy so they satiate you well, and they're quite flexible in the hands of a good home cook. You can cut them out in any shape imaginable. You can fry, roast, bake, or boil them. You can mash them to your heart's desire. And of course, you can cook them in your air fryer. Enjoy your potatoes for breakfast, perhaps with some sunny side up eggs.

These starchy tubers are excellent sources of vitamin B6, vitamin C, potassium and manganese. Also, they're very low in saturated fat and sodium. You got to love potatoes!

Ingredients:

- 2 Russet potatoes, chopped
- 2 teaspoons olive oil
- ¼ teaspoon salt
- ⅛ teaspoon black pepper
- 1 small onion, chopped

Directions:

1. Pre-heat the air fryer to 400 F.
2. Toss the chopped potatoes in olive oil, and season with salt and pepper.
3. Place inside the basket of the air fryer and roast for 10 minutes.
4. Open the basket and add in the chopped onion and cook for another 10 minutes or until golden brown with crunchy edges.
5. Transfer to a serving platter, and serve. Top with sunny side up eggs (optional).

Nutritional Info (per serving):

- ✓ Calories – 101
- ✓ Fat – 2.5 g
- ✓ Fiber – 3.0 g
- ✓ Carbs – 18.4 g
- ✓ Protein – 2.0 g
- ✓ Sodium – 154 mg

Potato Pancakes

Prep time: 10 min | **Cooking time**: 24 min | **Servings** 4

Another dish of potatoes is potato pancakes. With a fried crispy crust, they just melt in your mouth.

Ingredients:

- 1 medium sized onion, finely chopped
- 4 medium sized potatoes, cleaned and peeled
- 1 egg, beaten
- ¼ cup of milk
- 3 tablespoons of all-purpose flour
- ¼ teaspoon of kosher salt
- ½ teaspoon of garlic powder
- 2 tablespoons of unsalted butter
- Ground black pepper to taste

Directions:

1. Take the peeled potatoes and gently shred them up and place them in a bowl.
2. Add cold water and wash them. Wash them until the starch is washed off them.
3. Take a kitchen towel and wash off the starch. Drain your potatoes using a kitchen towel.
4. In a mixing bowl add egg, milk, butter, pepper, garlic powder, and salt.
5. Add the flour and your shredded potatoes. Mix the batter.
6. Pre-heat your Air Fryer to a temperature of 390°Fahrenheit (200°C).
7. Take out your cooking basket and cook them for about ¼ cup of potato pancake batter for about 12 minutes.
8. Once they have a brown texture, it is time to serve them!

Nutritional Info (per serving):

- ✓ Calories – 255
- ✓ Fat – 7.5 g
- ✓ Fiber – 5.9 g
- ✓ Carbs – 41.68 g
- ✓ Protein – 6.5 g
- ✓ Sodium – 225 mg

Spinach & Feta Frittata

Prep time: 5 min | **Cooking time**: 15 min | **Servings** 4

Start your day with the right level of energy. This Greek-inspired frittata will provide you that breakfast that's both filling and healthy.

Spinach is an extremely nutritious-packed vegetable, rich in vitamin K, vitamin A, vitamin C, magnesium, iron, potassium, and many more. Plus, the feta cheese imparts a slightly tart flavor without that much fat as in other harder cheeses.

This is perhaps one of the easiest meals you can prepare in your air fryer, guaranteed to give you a stress-free morning.

Ingredients:

- 4 eggs
- 2 cups spinach leaves
- ¼ cup of feta cheese, crumbled
- ¼ teaspoon salt
- ⅛ teaspoon black pepper

Directions:

1. Pre-heat the air fryer at 360 F.
2. Whisk the eggs in a bowl and season with salt and black pepper.
3. Add the spinach and feta cheese into the whisked eggs. Blend well.
4. Pour the egg mixture into the baking accessory, or into a separate shallow pan that can fit the air fryer. Cook for 5 minutes.
5. Carefully remove from the baking accessory and transfer to a serving plate.
6. Serve.

Nutritional Info (per serving):

- ✓ Calories – 90.0
- ✓ Fat – 6.4 g
- ✓ Fiber – 0.2 g
- ✓ Carbs – 1.0 g
- ✓ Protein – 7.1 g
- ✓ Sodium – 320 mg

Strawberry Cream Cheese Toasts

Prep time: 5 min | **Cooking time**: 5 min | **Servings** 4

A toast is a toast, but this simple toast can transform your morning from ordinary to extraordinary. Using an air fryer, you can make the crunchiest toasts ever. Add to that a delightful flavor combo of strawberries and cream cheese, and you have a winning toast.

Try this recipe and discover how easy it is to make fabulous toasts using your air fryer. This recipe calls for healthy ingredients which you probably already have at home. If not, it's to start your path in choosing better options when eating.

Ingredients:

- 4 slices whole wheat bread
- 4 tablespoons reduced-fat cream cheese
- 1 teaspoon honey
- 4 tablespoons strawberry jam

Directions:

1. Pre-heat the air fryer to 400 F.
2. Combine cream cheese and honey together and mix well.
3. Spread evenly over the 4 slices of bread
4. Place inside the air fryer and toast the bread for 5 minutes.
5. Serve with a layer of strawberry jam on top. You may also opt to top it with slices of fresh strawberries.

Nutritional Info (per serving):

- ✓ Calories – 181
- ✓ Fat – 4.5 g
- ✓ Fiber – 2.0 g
- ✓ Carbs – 32.8 g
- ✓ Protein – 3.8 g
- ✓ Sodium – 180 mg

Breakfast Bagel Sandwich

Prep time: 5 min | **Cooking time**: 10 min | **Servings** 1

Do you sometimes feel that you're too busy that even making your own sandwich can be a chore? The next thing you know, you're off to your favorite deli or café to buy a ready-to-eat bagel sandwich.

But wait. With an air fryer, you may just change your mind.

Here's a simple recipe to try this weekend for your post-workout, or just something to fill you up on a lazy day. Do yourself a favor and go for the whole wheat bagel to add more fiber to your diet.

Ingredients:

- 1 piece (40g) whole wheat bagel
- 2 eggs
- 1 slice of smoked, fat-free ham
- ⅛ teaspoon black pepper

Directions:

1. Pre-heat the air fryer to 370 F.
2. Slice the bagel in half, then toast both sides in the air fryer for 2 minutes or until golden brown. Set aside.
3. Place the slice of ham in the air fryer and cook for about 2 minutes. Set aside.
4. Whisk the eggs in a bowl, season with black pepper, and cook in the air fryer for about 2-3 minutes or until done.
5. Assemble the sandwich. Don't forget to pair with your favorite coffee or some tea.

Nutritional Info (per serving):

- ✓ Calories – 238
- ✓ Fat – 9.4 g
- ✓ Fiber – 3.1 g
- ✓ Carbs – 21.2 g
- ✓ Protein – 17.5 g
- ✓ Sodium – 477 mg

Banana Bread

Prep time: 15 min | **Cooking time**: 25 min | **Servings** 8

Baking a loaf of banana bread using your air fryer is such a breeze. It's like having your own convection oven, but way simpler. Plan your week ahead and make banana bread when you have some time to tinker with your air fryer.

This recipe is a quick pop-in-and-want kind of baked goodie, which can be served for breakfast to pair with your favorite morning brew.

Plus, it's a smart way to use those extra, overripe bananas at home. Bananas are excellent sources of potassium and fiber, so you can be use you're doing your body a big flavor.

Ingredients:

- 1 ½ cups all-purpose flour
- 2 ¼ teaspoon baking powder
- ¾ teaspoon salt
- ¼ teaspoon baking soda
- ½ teaspoon cinnamon powder
- ⅓ cup unsalted butter
- ⅔ cup brown sugar, unpacked
- 2 medium eggs
- ½ teaspoon vanilla extract
- 3 ripe medium-sized bananas, mashed

Directions:

1. Pre-heat the air fryer to 350 F.
2. Grease a baking pan that will fit your air fryer.
3. In a mixing bowl, combine all dry ingredients: all-purpose flour, baking powder, salt, baking soda, and cinnamon powder. Set aside.
4. In another bowl, cream the butter and brown sugar. Gradually add the eggs and vanilla, then blend together until smooth.
5. Add in the dry ingredients until you form a soft batter.
6. Add the mashed bananas to the batter, and stir until the bananas are well distributed in the batter.
7. Transfer the batter to the greased baking pan.
8. Place in the air fryer and bake for 20 minutes.
9. Insert a toothpick to check if its' done. Once toothpick comes out dry, take out the baking pan and let cool for about 10 minutes.
10. Remove the banana bread from the baking pan, slice, and serve.

Nutritional Info (per serving):

- ✓ Calories – 227
- ✓ Fat – 8.9 g
- ✓ Fiber – 2.1 g
- ✓ Carbs – 34.5 g
- ✓ Protein – 3.6 g
- ✓ Sodium – 330 mg

Breakfast Sausages

Prep time: 5 min | **Cooking time**: 20 min | **Servings** 4

Air frying breakfast sausages is another option you can do with this wonder kitchen appliance. Use any of your favorite breakfast sausages and cook oil-free using your air fryer.

In this recipe, we'll also make some quick mashed potatoes to pair with your breakfast sausages. This tandem will provide you adequate carbohydrates and protein to start your day.

Don't forget some fresh fruits on the side or a fresh pressed juice, and you'll have this perfect breakfast in just a few simple steps.

Ingredients:

- 4 pieces lean breakfast sausages, fresh
- 2 large potato, peeled and cubed
- 1 small carrot, peeled and minced
- ½ cup reduced fat 2% milk
- 1 tablespoon unsalted butter, left at room temperature
- ⅛ teaspoon salt
- ⅛ teaspoon black pepper

Directions:

1. Pre-heat the air fryer to 400 F.
2. Place the breakfast sausages in the air fryer, along with the cubed potatoes on the side. Cook for 15 minutes.
3. Open the basket and take out the cooked potato cubes.
4. In a bowl, mash the potato cubes and add the carrots, milk, butter, salt and black pepper. Mix well.
5. Place the mashed potatoes back in the air fryer with the sausages and cook for another 5 minutes.
6. Transfer to a serving dish, and serve.

Nutritional Info (per serving):

- ✓ Calories – 280
- ✓ Fat – 13.4 g
- ✓ Fiber – 1.5 g
- ✓ Carbs – 20.4 g
- ✓ Protein – 19.7 g
- ✓ Sodium – 101 mg

Fried Baked Eggs

Prep time: 2 min | **Cooking time**: 6 min | **Servings** 4

This original toast can be decorated with green onions or parsley. It can serve as an excellent addition to various salads.

Ingredients:

- 4 tablespoons of herbs, chopped such as tarragon, parsley, and chives
- 4 pieces of crusty dinner rolls
- 4 tablespoons of heavy cream
- Pepper to taste
- Salt to taste
- Parmesan cheese, grated
- 4 eggs

Directions:

1. Slice the top of your dinner rolls and gently remove the bread inside of the roll, until there is a hole within large enough to hold an egg.
2. Arrange the rolls in your Air Fryer cooking basket.
3. Crack an egg into each of the rolls and top them with some assorted herbs.
4. Add a bit of cream onto them along with salt and pepper. Sprinkle the tops with parmesan.
5. Air Fry them for about 6 minutes at 350°Fahrenheit (176°C).
6. Let them rest inside for about 5 minutes, serve warm!

Nutritional Info (per serving):

- ✓ Calories – 171
- ✓ Fat – 10.0 g
- ✓ Fiber – 1.0 g
- ✓ Carbs – 10.5 g
- ✓ Protein – 8.0 g
- ✓ Sodium – 320 mg

Air Fryer Vegetables & Side Dishes Recipes

Sweet Potato Chips

Prep time: 5 min | **Cooking time**: 10 min | **Servings** 4

If you're looking for the best snack to nibble as you journey towards healthy eating, sweet potatoes should be at the top of your list.

Seriously, these lowly tubers deserve your full attention. Sweet potatoes will give you a better vision of life. Literally. A serving of 100g provides 283% of the RDA for Vitamin A. That's a lot of beta carotene to give some TLC to your eyes.

The air fryer loves the sweet potato - together they make the crispiest chips you can ever imagine.

Ingredients:

- 500g sweet potatoes
- 3 tablespoons olive oil
- ¼ teaspoon cinnamon
- ⅛ teaspoon chili powder
- ⅛ teaspoon salt
- ⅛ teaspoon black pepper

Directions:

1. Pre-heat the air fryer to 350 F.
2. Slice the sweet potato into thin chips using a mandolin.
3. Drizzle the sweet potato chips in olive oil, and sprinkle the cinnamon, salt, and black pepper. Toss until well blended.
4. Place the chips in the air fryer basket and cook for 10 minutes, shaking midway in the cooking.
5. Once crisp and golden brown, transfer to a bowl.
6. Serve.

Nutritional Info (per serving):

- ✓ Calories – 238
- ✓ Fat – 10.7 g
- ✓ Fiber – 5.3 g
- ✓ Carbs – 35.1 g
- ✓ Protein – 1.9 g
- ✓ Sodium – 86 mg

Baked Baby Potatoes

Prep time: 5 min | **Cooking time**: 10 min | **Servings** 2

Here's another simple way to enjoy your favorite baby potatoes, a.k.a. marble potatoes. Using an air fryer, you can easily roast them to perfection. You don't need fancy ingredients; just the simplest seasonings will bring out the roasted potato flavor many people love.

Baby potatoes are fun to eat and make a good pairing with different entrees like meat and poultry.

They're best roasted with your favorite herbs and seasonings to add some flavor to its neutral taste.

Ingredients:

- 250 g baby potatoes, halved
- 1 teaspoon olive oil
- ¼ teaspoon oregano powder
- ⅛ teaspoon garlic powder
- ⅛ teaspoon dried thyme
- ⅛ teaspoon salt
- ⅛ teaspoon black pepper

Directions:

1. Pre-heat the air fryer to 350 F.
2. Wash the baby potatoes and cut them in halves.
3. Toss the halved baby potatoes in olive oil, oregano, garlic powder, thyme, salt, and pepper.
4. Place the baby potatoes in the baking accessory and roast for 10 minutes.
5. Shake the baby potatoes midway at 5 minutes to ensure all parts become crispy.
6. Transfer the roasted potatoes to a serving dish, and serve.

Nutritional Info (per serving):

- ✓ Calories – 94
- ✓ Fat – 2.5 g
- ✓ Fiber – 3.3 g
- ✓ Carbs – 15.9 g
- ✓ Protein – 3.3 g
- ✓ Sodium – 71 mg

Roasted Brussel Sprouts and Butternut Squash

Prep time: 5 min | **Cooking time**: 15 min | **Servings** 4

If you're looking for something warm and comforting, some roasted vegetables can do just that. Roasting is simple to do in an air fryer and these vegetables will roast quite well.

In this recipe, we combine Brussel sprouts with butternut squash for an amazing flavor tandem. Who knows? This dish may even bring out some of your most special memories of autumn.

Brussel sprouts are high in protein, rich in vitamin K and vitamin C, and help improve bone health and manage diabetes. Not to be outdone, butternut squash boasts of having very little saturated fat, cholesterol and sodium, and is equally nutrient-dense. Talk about being the most popular winter squash!

Ingredients:

- 2 cups (200g) Brussels sprouts, trimmed and halved
- 1 cup (250g) butternut squash, cubed
- 1 tablespoon honey
- 1 tablespoon balsamic vinegar
- 1 ½ tablespoons extra virgin olive oil
- ¼ teaspoon cinnamon powder
- ¼ teaspoon salt
- ¼ teaspoon black pepper

Directions:

1. Pre-heat the air fryer to 400 F.
2. In a large mixing bowl, combine Brussels sprouts and butternut squash.
3. Drizzle 1 tablespoon of olive oil over the vegetables and toss until it coats thoroughly. Season with salt and pepper.
4. Place in the air fryer basket and cook for 7 minutes.
5. Open the basket and mix the vegetables to ensure even cooking. Cook for another 7-8 minutes.
6. Meanwhile, prepare the dressing. Combine ½ tablespoon olive oil, honey, balsamic vinegar, cinnamon power and whisk until well blended.
7. Remove the vegetables from the air fryer and transfer to a mixing bowl. Drizzle the dressing over the roasted vegetables and toss until mixed thoroughly.
8. Transfer to a serving container and serve.

Nutritional Info (per serving):

- ✓ Calories – 82
- ✓ Fat – 3.7 g
- ✓ Fiber – 2.4 g
- ✓ Carbs – 12.5 g
- ✓ Protein – 1.9 g
- ✓ Sodium – 160 mg

French Fries

Prep time: 5 min + 30 min soaking | **Cooking time**: 20 min | **Servings** 4

One of the best application of the air fryer is making French fries. In fact, many people are introduced to the air fryer via perfectly crisp French fries minus the dunking in traditional deep-fryers.

With the air fryer's basket, it's almost like the air fryer was invented to help you prepare the healthiest French fries you can possibly have. You can enjoy that satisfying fried taste without the oil. If you're controlling your fat intake, this is one of the best and healthiest side dishes or snacks you should have in your diet plan.

Here's what's even better. You can have them in the comfort of your own home anytime you feel like having French fries! Goodbye, fast food. It's time to air fry some French fries and enjoy that crisp texture without any of that guilt.

Ingredients:

- 2 large Russet potatoes
- 1 tablespoon fresh parsley, chopped
- 2 teaspoons vegetable oil
- ¼ teaspoon sea salt

Directions:

1. Pre-heat the air fryer to 330 F.
2. Prepare the potatoes by washing them thoroughly, using a brush to scrub the skin.
3. Hand cut the potatoes into French-fry strips, or use a vegetable slicer that allows you to make this easily. You may opt to leave the skin on or choose to peel it.
4. Soak the potatoes in water for 30 minutes.
5. After 30 minutes, drain the potatoes well. Use paper towels to pat them dry.
6. Add a small amount (about a teaspoon or two) of oil to the potatoes, and mix well until the oil coats the potatoes.
7. Place the potatoes in the basket and pre-cook for 5 minutes.
8. Allow to cool.
9. Further, add salt to pre-cooked fries and cook for another 15 minutes. To make it flavorful add chopped parsley at the end of cooking.
10. Remove from the basket and serve.

Nutritional Info (per serving):

- ✓ Calories – 94
- ✓ Fat – 2.4 g
- ✓ Fiber – 2.6 g
- ✓ Carbs – 16.8 g
- ✓ Protein – 1.8 g
- ✓ Sodium – 38 mg

Zucchini Ricotta Puffs

Prep time: 10 min | **Cooking time**: 10 min | **Servings** 4

When we talk about puff pastry, we imagine a delectable piece of dessert or savory snack that's crunchy and flaky. It's often used with sweet or savory fillings and baked in the oven until you get that nice, golden brown color and crunchy texture.

In this recipe, you'll have veggies as your filling. We're using zucchini and basil to boost your body with vitamins and minerals. To add a little bit of creaminess, we added some ricotta to make the texture even more exciting. The contrast between crunchy and creamy will create a fun experience in your mouth.

So get ready and start making these puff pastry treats using your air fryer. Remember, your air fryer does not only fry but also bakes too!

Ingredients:

- 1 sheet ready-made puff pastry
- ⅛ cup fresh mill for glazing

Filling:

- 1 cup ricotta cheese
- 1 zucchini, diced
- ½ cup basil leaves, shredded
- Salt & pepper

Directions:

1. Pre-heat the air fryer to 390 F.
2. Prepare the filling by combining zucchini, basil leaves, ricotta cheese, salt, and pepper. Mix well and set aside.
3. Cut the puff pastry sheet into 16 small squares.
4. Scoop the filling onto each square then fold over to form a triangle. Seal the edges by pressing them together
5. Place the filled puff pastries into the basket.
6. Using a pastry brush spread a layer of milk over the filled puff pastries.
7. Bake the puff pastries in 10 minutes.
8. Remove from the basket and transfer to a serving dish.
9. Serve.

Nutritional Info (per serving):

- ✓ Calories – 258
- ✓ Fat – 15.2 g
- ✓ Fiber – 1.6 g
- ✓ Carbs – 21.3 g
- ✓ Protein – 11.0 g
- ✓ Sodium – 226 mg

Crispy Sesame Tofu Bites

Prep time: 5 min | **Cooking time**: 20 min | **Servings** 4

Tofu has become so popular among the community of healthy eaters since it's a great source of non-meat protein.

If you prefer not to have meat in your dishes, tofu is an awesome replacement. Mind you, the tofu is not a second rate citizen in the food world. Tofu is a big time player when it comes to nutrition.

Aside from being an excellent source of protein, it will give you the essential amino acids, all eight of them. Plus, it has iron and calcium to help improve your bone health, and minerals like manganese, selenium and phosphorous.

Ingredients:

- 500g tofu, firm or semi-firm
- 2 teaspoons toasted sesame seeds

Dipping sauce:

- 1 tablespoon light soy sauce
- ½ teaspoon sesame oil
- 2 cloves garlic, minced
- 1 tablespoon chopped scallions

Directions:

1. Pre-heat the air fryer to 350 F.
2. Cut the tofu block into cubes, approximately 1 inch cubes.
3. Place the tofu cubes in the basket and cook for 10 minutes.
4. Meanwhile, prepare the dipping sauce. Combine soy sauce, sesame oil, garlic and scallions together and mix well.
5. Open the basket after 10 minutes, shake to toss the tofu cubes, and cook for another 10 minutes or until golden brown.
6. Transfer the cooked tofu to a serving platter and sprinkle with toasted sesame seeds.
7. Serve with the dipping sauce.

Nutritional Info (per serving):

- ✓ Calories – 96
- ✓ Fat – 4.7 g
- ✓ Fiber – 0.4 g
- ✓ Carbs – 4.0 g
- ✓ Protein – 9.5 g
- ✓ Sodium – 276 mg

Eggplant Chips

Prep time: 5 min | **Cooking time**: 7-10 min | **Servings** 4

Since the air fryer is a pro when it comes to making chips, we have another recipe involving chips. This time, we're using eggplant.

Like any vegetable, eggplants are a good staple in your diet. It's fleshy, and you can grill, roast, bake, boil, mash, add to stews, add to pastas, or like this recipe, make it into a side dish.

If you're trying to lose weight, add more vegetables when you plan your menu. Eggplants have fiber, manganese, folate, potassium, and an array of vitamins and minerals. You need all these to keep your body glowing.

Ingredients:

- 2 large eggplants, sliced into 1 cm-chips
- 1 teaspoon extra virgin olive oil
- 100 g pomegranate seeds (optional)
- 1 tablespoon alfalfa sprouts (optional)
- ⅛ teaspoon sea salt
- ⅛ teaspoon black pepper
- 100 g plain Greek yogurt

Directions:

1. Pre-heat the air fryer to 390 F
2. Slice the eggplant into chips, approximately 1 cm thick.
3. Place the eggplant chips in a mixing bowl. Drizzle olive oil on the eggplant, and season with salt & pepper.
4. Arrange the eggplant chips in the basket, and air fry for 7 minutes or until desired doneness.
5. Remove from the air fryer and arrange on a serving platter. Top with some Greek yogurt.
6. You may opt to add some pomegranate seeds and alfalfa sprouts as garnish.
7. Serve.

Nutritional Info (per serving):

- ✓ Calories – 116
- ✓ Fat – 2.4 g
- ✓ Fiber – 10.5 g
- ✓ Carbs – 17.4 g
- ✓ Protein – 5.5 g
- ✓ Sodium – 73 mg

Roasted Florets

Prep time: 5 min | **Cooking time**: 10-15 min | **Servings** 4

If you're looking for some side dish for your dinner tonight, you can try this roasted medley of vegetables. It's quick and easy to do, and you can even roast them in your air fryer along with your steak. That way, you can save time and energy.

In this recipe, we use a trio of broccoli, cauliflower and carrots. All these vegetables are guaranteed health boosters while making your dish quite pretty too. Just look at that lovely combination of colors and you know what I mean.

The most basic seasonings are used to bring out the true flavor goodness of these vegetables. When you have fresh vegetables on hand, it's best to preserve their nutrients and roasting is the way to you.

Ingredients:

- 250 g broccoli
- 250 g cauliflower
- 100 g carrot
- 1 tablespoon olive oil
- ¼ teaspoon garlic powder
- ¼ teaspoon sea salt
- ⅛ teaspoon black pepper

Directions:

1. Preheat the air fryer to 390 F.
2. Wash the vegetables and cut into bite- sized pieces. Pat dry.
3. In a bowl, season the cut vegetables with olive oil, garlic powder, sea salt, and black pepper.
4. Place the seasoned vegetables in the air fryer and roast for 10 minutes.
5. Check for doneness, or roast for an additional 5 minutes or less.
6. Transfer the roasted vegetables in a serving plate and serve warm.

Nutritional Info (per serving):

- ✓ Calories – 78
- ✓ Fat – 3.8 g
- ✓ Fiber – 3.8 g
- ✓ Carbs – 10.1 g
- ✓ Protein – 3.2 g
- ✓ Sodium – 174 mg

Baked Corn

Prep time: 5 min | **Cooking time**: 10 min | **Servings** 4

Here's another side dish that you can easily prepare using your air fryer –baked corn. The air fryer's basket is quite handy to use as a container for cut up cobs of corn or you can bake them as whole ears of corn if they fit in your air fryer.

You may opt to bake your corn shredded, possibly along with carrots and peas, but this recipe will teach you the basic of cooking whole ears of corn.

Once baked, you can pair them with your baked ribs or steaks or simply eat them on their own as a healthy, fiber-rich snack.

Ingredients:

- 4 ears of corn
- 2 tablespoon olive oil
- ¼ teaspoon garlic powder
- ¼ teaspoon onion powder
- ¼ teaspoon salt
- ⅛ teaspoon black pepper

Directions:

1. Pre-heat the air fryer to 390 F.
2. Remove the husks and silk from the corn, and wash.
3. Depending on the size of your corn and basket, cut the corn as needed to fit your container.
4. Coat the corn with olive oil, then sprinkle garlic powder, onion powder, salt and pepper all over.
5. Place the corn in the air fryer basket and roast for 10 minutes. Rotate the corn halfway through cooking.
6. Remove from the basket and serve.

Nutritional Info (per serving):

- ✓ Calories – 193
- ✓ Fat – 8.8 g
- ✓ Fiber – 4.3 g
- ✓ Carbs – 29.3 g
- ✓ Protein – 5.1 g
- ✓ Sodium – 170 mg

Taro Batonnet

Prep time: 5 min | **Cooking time**: 20 min | **Servings** 4

Taro is a starchy vegetable like its cousin potato, but with even more fiber – twice! It's quite popular among the health-conscious circles as it's also a good source of vitamin B-6, vitamin C, magnesium, folate and potassium.

For this recipe, we cut the taro into batonnet, a French vegetable cut that looks like a "baton" or stick. You may also use a different cut, like the more common chips or wedges. Just make sure the pieces are uniformly cut, as much as possible, for even cooking.

Air frying taro makes it crunchy outside, but still tender and soft inside. Use as an appetizer with ketchup or mayo, or as a side dish to roasted or grilled meats, poultry or fish.

Ingredients:

- 2 cups taro, peeled, bayonet cut
- 1 teaspoon olive oil
- ⅛ teaspoon salt
- ⅛ teaspoon black pepper

Directions:

1. Pre-heat the air fryer to 360 F.
2. In a mixing bowl, season with taro with salt and black pepper. Drizzle with olive oil and coal evenly.
3. Place the taro in the basket and air fry for 20 minutes. Halfway into the cooking, shake the basket to loosen the taro pieces and cook evenly.
4. Transfer to a serving platter, and serve hot as an appetizer or as side dish to your entrée.

Nutritional Info (per serving):

- ✓ Calories – 88
- ✓ Fat – 3.6 g
- ✓ Fiber – 2.2 g
- ✓ Carbs – 13.8 g
- ✓ Protein – 0.8 g
- ✓ Sodium – 153 mg

Crispy Onion Rings

Prep time: 5 min + 30 min soaking | **Cooking time**: 8-10 min | **Servings** 4

Onion rings are like French fries for adults. With the right way of preparing onion rings, you'll get that nice sweet flavor from this vegetable, plus all those nutrients too.

Here's why you shouldn't take onions for granted. Onions have phytochemicals as well as vitamin C which help in improving your body's immunity.

This recipe calls for some buttermilk to soak your onions in, adding moisture to keep them moist while frying. With an air fryer, frying onion rings have become hassle-free. None of those possible hot oil splatter as you deep fry the onions. What a relief!

Ingredients:

- 1 large sweet onion, cut into rings 1 cm wide
- 2 cups buttermilk, low cultured fat
- 1 cup all-purpose flour
- ¼ teaspoon salt
- ⅛ teaspoon black pepper

Directions:

1. Pre-heat the air fryer to 375 F.
2. Soak the onion rings in buttermilk for at least 30 minutes.
3. Meanwhile, combine the flour, salt, and black pepper in a shallow bowl.
4. Take the soaked onion rings, a few pieces at a time, and toss them into the seasoned flour until well coated.
5. Place them in the air fryer and cook for 8-10 minutes, or until golden brown.
6. Transfer to a serving platter.

Nutritional Info (per serving):

- ✓ Calories – 189
- ✓ Fat – 1.5 g
- ✓ Fiber – 1.6 g
- ✓ Carbs – 36.0 g
- ✓ Protein – 7.9 g
- ✓ Sodium – 283 mg

Air Fryer Chicken Recipes

Lemon & Garlic Chicken

Prep time: 15 min + marinating 30 min | **Cooking time**: 30 min | **Servings** 4

This mouthwatering dish will tempt even the most discerning diners who require a healthy, satisfying meal without the greasy aftertaste often found in conventional fried foods. The lemon can be replaced with any other fruit such as orange, mango, pineapple or apricots for an unusual variation. Perfect for a quick meal with little washing up.

Ingredients:

- 4 fresh organic Chicken Legs, Skin on, Thigh included
- 1 large Lemon, sliced into rings (or any other fruit you may wish to use)
- 4 tbsp of Ghee
- 2 tbsp of Coconut or Olive Oil
- 2 tbsp of dried Oregano
- 1 tbsp of dried Rosemary
- 2 tbsp of Fresh Lemon Juice (or other fruit juice)
- 1 tsp of smoked and dried Paprika
- 4 cloves of minced Garlic
- Sea Salt and freshly cracked Black Pepper to taste

Directions:

1. Place the ghee, coconut oil, oregano, rosemary, fruit juice, paprika, garlic, salt and pepper in a food safe, an airtight container such as a zip-lock bag or large glass jar.
2. Add the chicken legs and stir or shake it for a few minutes, so the chicken is well covered in marinade.
3. Place it in the fridge for at least 30 minutes (or as long as 24 hours) for the flavors to infuse.
4. Oil the tray or basket of your air fry oven and turn it on to preheat to 350F.
5. Place the marinated chicken legs in the basket/tray.
6. Place the slices of lemon on and between the chicken legs.
7. Cook in the air fryer for 30 minutes or until golden brown.
8. Remove the chicken legs in the tray and allow them to stand for 5 to 10 minutes to rest before serving.

Nutritional Info (per serving):

- ✓ Calories – 446
- ✓ Fat – 26.9 g
- ✓ Fiber – 2.0 g
- ✓ Carbs – 4.8 g
- ✓ Protein – 46 g
- ✓ Sodium – 116 mg

Air Fried Chicken Wings

Prep time: 5 min | **Cooking time**: 10 min | **Servings** 4

Who doesn't love chicken wings? When cooked to a crisp, they're fun to eat while you watch the game with family or friends. But come on, even if these wings are not too crisp, they're still awfully good.

In this recipe, you'll learn how to prepare air fried chicken wings using some basic ingredients.

Are you ready to air fryer some mean wings? Let's do it!

Ingredients:

- 8 chicken wings (8 drumettes + 8 wingettes)
- ½ teaspoon smoked paprika
- 2 tablespoon light barbecue sauce
- ½ teaspoon cayenne pepper
- 2 cloves garlic, minced
- ⅛ teaspoon black pepper

Directions:

1. Pre-heat the air fryer to 350 F.
2. Combine all the herbs and spices, then rub the mixture to the chicken wings.
3. Place the chicken wings in the basket.
4. Roast the chicken wings for 10 minutes or until crispy brown.
5. Serve as is or with some sauce.

Nutritional Info (per serving):

- ✓ Calories – 331
- ✓ Fat – 21.5 g
- ✓ Fiber – 0.5 g
- ✓ Carbs – 14.0 g
- ✓ Protein – 19.7 g
- ✓ Sodium – 484 mg

Rosemary Chicken Drumsticks

Prep time: 5 min + 30 min marinating | **Cooking time**: 15 min | **Servings** 4

This recipe focuses the spotlight on the herb that's perhaps most often associated with chicken. Rosemary is an herb that has both antibacterial and antioxidant properties. In other words, it helps your body prevent and fight infections and reduce cell damage.

Make it a habit to cook with herbs, all kinds of herbs if you will to maximize the benefits of each one of them. Different herbs have different properties.

We use drumsticks in this recipe, but you can use other parts as well. We also removed the chicken skin and added a healthier kind of fat – olive oil. This way, we keep out the bad fats out and maintain the good ones.

Ingredients:

- 4 chicken drumsticks, skinless
- 1 teaspoon olive oil
- 2 tablespoon cider vinegar
- ½ teaspoon garlic powder
- ½ teaspoon dried rosemary
- ⅛ teaspoon sea salt
- ⅛ teaspoon black pepper

Directions:

1. Pre-heat the air fryer to 400 F.
2. Marinate the chicken in olive oil, balsamic vinegar, garlic powder, dried rosemary, sea salt, and black pepper for at least 30 minutes in the refrigerator.
3. Transfer the chicken drumsticks to the air fryer's basket and cook for 15 minutes.
4. Once cooked, place the chicken on a serving dish and serve with a side salad.

Nutritional Info (per serving):

- ✓ Calories – 91
- ✓ Fat – 3.8 g
- ✓ Fiber – 0.1 g
- ✓ Carbs – 0.4 g
- ✓ Protein – 12.7 g
- ✓ Sodium – 53 mg

Lemon Parmesan Chicken Wings

Prep time: 5 min | **Cooking time**: 10-15 min | **Servings** 4

This recipe for lemon Parmesan is an adaptation of other recipes that call for air frying chicken wings. As you know, the air fryer's expertise is frying food fast and easy without the oil.

So here, we flavored the chicken wings with lemon for that citrus note. Lemon is essential for your nutrition as it helps reduce the acidity in your body. It's an effective antioxidant too.

For coating, we embrace the chicken wings with grated Parmesan instead of the usual flour or potato starch. The air fried Parmesan will turn crispy brown to give your mouth that much-desired crunch.

Ingredients:

- 12 chicken wings (12 drumettes + 12 wingettes), raw
- 1 lemon (juice)
- 3 tablespoons reduced-fat, grated Parmesan
- ¼ teaspoon garlic powder
- ⅛ teaspoon sea salt
- ⅛ teaspoon black pepper

Directions:

1. Pre-heat the air fryer to 360 F.
2. Season the grated Parmesan with garlic powder, sea salt, and black pepper.
3. Meanwhile, squeeze 1 lemon over the chicken wings and mix well.
4. Coat each chicken wing in the Parmesan mixture.
5. Transfer all the coated chicken wings to the air fryer basket and air fry for 10-15 minutes.
6. Once cooked to desired doneness, place the chicken wings on a serving dish and serve hot.

Nutritional Info (per serving):

- ✓ Calories – 299
- ✓ Fat – 19.8 g
- ✓ Fiber – 0.7 g
- ✓ Carbs – 11.2 g
- ✓ Protein – 1.8 g
- ✓ Sodium – 372 mg

Honey Sriracha Wings

Prep time: 5 min | **Cooking time**: 20 min | **Servings** 4

Honey Sriracha Wings is a recipe you can do using your air fryer especially when you need some appetizers. The sweet-spice combination will surely what anyone's appetite and prepare for them for the main course.

In this recipe, you'll be using Sriracha sauce, essentially a type of chili sauce named after the city of Si Racha in Thailand. If you have other preferred hot sauces, by all means, use them and substitute easily. Or you can adjust the quantity to make it milder or hotter!

Here's some good news. Chili peppers have capsaicin, a compound that's known to have analgesic properties. Moreover, chili peppers contain antioxidants like vitamin C and carotenoids. Studies show chili peppers can help reduce the damaging effects of bad cholesterol.

Ingredients:

- 12 chicken wings (12 drumettes + 12 wingettes)
- 1 tablespoon Sriracha sauce
- 1 tablespoon honey
- 1 teaspoon sesame seeds for garnish
- ½ teaspoon sesame oil
- ¼ teaspoon sea salt
- ⅛ teaspoon black pepper

Directions:

1. Pre-heat the air fryer to 400 F.
2. Rinse and pat dry chicken wings.
3. Season with sea salt and black pepper.
4. Place in the air fryer basket and fry for 20 minutes.
5. Open the basket midway of cooking period to flip the chicken wings.
6. Transfer the air fried chicken wings to a mixing bowl and toss with the Sriracha sauce, honey, and sesame oil.
7. Serve and top with sesame seeds.

Nutritional Info (per serving):

- ✓ Calories – 53
- ✓ Fat – 2.5 g
- ✓ Fiber – 0.1 g
- ✓ Carbs – 6.1 g
- ✓ Protein – 1.6 g
- ✓ Sodium – 246 mg

Chicken Spring Roll

Prep time: 20 min | **Cooking time**: 5 min | **Servings** 4

Spring rolls are quite popular with the influx of Asian-inspired dishes globally. Usually, pork is used as part of the filling. In this recipe, we'll be using chicken instead of pork to make it a healthier alternative.

Using an air fryer to make this dish is even beneficial as it cut downs the oil and cooking time. In no time, you can have crispy spring rolls at home.

The chicken breast will give your protein, while the added carrot and celery will provide you essential vitamins and minerals.

Ingredients:

- 100g chicken breast, pre-boiled
- 1 celery stalk
- 1 medium-sized carrot
- ¼ teaspoon onion powder
- ⅛ teaspoon ground black pepper
- ⅛ teaspoon salt
- 8 spring roll wrappers
- 1 teaspoon cornstarch
- ⅛ cup water

Directions:

1. Pre-heat the air fryer to 400 F.
2. Shred the pre-boiled chicken breast. Set aside
3. Slice the celery stalk into thin strips about 1-2 inches long.
4. Similarly, slice the carrot into thin strips about 1-12 inches long.
5. Combine the shredded chicken breast, celery, carrots, onion powder, salt and black pepper to make the filling.
6. Prepare a cornstarch slurry by mixing cornstarch with water. Set aside.
7. Place about 2 tablespoons of filling onto each spring roll, then roll it up. Seal the ends using the cornstarch slurry.
8. Put the spring rolls into the basket, and cook for 5 minutes.
9. Place on a platter, and serve.

Nutritional Info (per serving):

- ✓ Calories – 225
- ✓ Fat – 1.6 g
- ✓ Fiber – 1.6 g
- ✓ Carbs – 39.5 g
- ✓ Protein – 11.8 g
- ✓ Sodium – 467 mg

Guilt-Free BBQ Wings

Prep time: 5 min | **Cooking time**: 15 min | **Servings** 4

Here's another variation of the chicken wings recipe to give you more options for your next party. This time, make it BBQ style.

The important thing is to learn and master creating the basic crispy chicken wings. From there, you can experiment and use other sauces of your choice. For now, use your favorite BBQ sauce to simplify.

By cooking your chicken wings in the air fryer, you cut down on fat, and that's more than enough reason to never fry using a deep-fryer ever again.

Ingredients:

- 12 chicken wings (12 drumettes + 12 wingettes)
- ½ cup buffalo sauce of your choice

Directions:

1. Pre-heat the air fryer to 400 F.
2. Rinse and pat dry the chicken wings before placing in the air fryer basket.
3. Air fry the wings for 7 minutes.
4. Open the basket, then shake and flip the wings. Return and cook for another 7-8 minutes or until crispy and golden brown.
5. Remove from the air fryer and transfer to a mixing bowl. Toss with the buffalo sauce of your choice.
6. Serve with some optional blue cheese dip.

Nutritional Info (per serving):

- ✓ Calories – 283
- ✓ Fat – 19 g
- ✓ Fiber – 0.3 g
- ✓ Carbs – 9.8 g
- ✓ Protein – 17.3 g
- ✓ Sodium – 397 mg

Baked Lemon Chicken Fillet

Prep time: 5 min | **Cooking time**: 13 min | **Servings** 4

It's almost time for dinner and nothing on the table. Don't panic. Here's a chicken dinner recipe that will take the stress out of your cooking.

With just a few ingredients, you can create a satisfying dish that's low in fat and high in protein. Since it's cooked in an air fryer, you can be sure to save time in the process.

This dish goes well with others, as you can pair it with some tomato or oil-based pasta. If you prefer to go light, have a big bowl of salad greens and place this chicken fillet on top. Squeeze a few more drops of lemon juice over your chicken for that extra tart flavor. What can be healthier than that?

Ingredients:

- 4 chicken breasts, raw
- 2 tablespoons olive oil
- 1 lemon juice
- ¼ teaspoon sea salt
- ⅛ teaspoon black pepper

Directions:

1. Pre-heat the air fryer to 390 F.
2. Mix the chicken breasts with olive oil and lemon juice until each part of the chicken is well marinated.
3. Season with salt and pepper.
4. Place the chicken breast fillets in the basket and cook for 13 minutes or until desired doneness.
5. Transfer to a serving dish, and serve. Add your favorite salad on the side.

Nutritional Info (per serving):

- ✓ Calories – 178
- ✓ Fat – 9.5 g
- ✓ Fiber – 0.4 g
- ✓ Carbs – 1.4 g
- ✓ Protein – 21.4 g
- ✓ Sodium – 168 mg

Honey Butter Wings

Prep time: 5 min | **Cooking time**: 20 min | **Servings** 4

There's a certain type of fun and playfulness in this flavor combination: honey and butter. Today, we'll flavor up our chicken wings, so you don't get stuck with the same old stuff.

But here's how we'll make it work with your healthy lifestyle. Use portion control properly. The secret? Don't skimp on flavor, but manage how much you eat.

Here's another tip. Load up on the salad. Indulge in these honey butter wings and gobble up a bowlful of healthy greens. Healthy living doesn't have to be rigid. Sometimes, you need to play a little bit more and enjoy every good food out there.

Ingredients:

- 12 chicken wings (12 drumettes + 12 wingettes), raw
- ½ cup cornstarch
- 1 tablespoon melted organic butter
- 2 tablespoon honey
- ⅛ teaspoon salt
- ⅛ teaspoon black pepper

Directions:

1. Pre-heat the air fryer to 360 F.
2. Rinse and pat dry the wings.
3. Combine the potato starch with salt and pepper. Coat the wings with this mixture.
4. Place the wings in the basket and cook for 10 minutes.
5. Flip the wings and cook for another 10 minutes or until crispy and golden brown.
6. In a mixing bowl, toss the cooked wings in honey and melted butter.
7. Transfer to a serving platter.

Nutritional Info (per serving):

- ✓ Calories – 427
- ✓ Fat – 25.0 g
- ✓ Fiber – 0.4 g
- ✓ Carbs – 32.8 g
- ✓ Protein – 17.4 g
- ✓ Sodium – 339 mg

Paprika & Pepper Sauce Wings

Prep time: 5 min | **Cooking time**: 20 min | **Servings** 4

Buffalo wings are the quintessential wings ever! They never go out of style, and it's always in season.

In this recipes, we'll use a combination of heat and fat. Use your favorite pepper sauce and if you can, go for unsalted butter.

Don't be afraid of butter! Here's how we'll make it work with your healthy lifestyle. Use portion control properly. The secret? Don't skimp on flavor, but manage how much you eat.

Here's another tip. Load up on the salad. Indulge in these paprika & pepper wings and gobble up a bowlful of healthy greens. Healthy living doesn't have to be rigid. Sometimes, you need to play a little bit more and enjoy every good food out there.

Ingredients:

- 12 chicken wings (12 drumettes + 12 wingettes), raw
- ¼ teaspoon paprika
- ¼ teaspoon garlic powder
- ⅛ teaspoon black pepper
- ¼ cup cayenne pepper sauce
- ¼ cup unsalted butter
- ¼ teaspoon salt

Directions:

1. Pre-heat the air fryer to 380 F.
2. Wash the chicken wings and pat dry.
3. Season with paprika, garlic powder, salt, & black pepper.
4. Place in the air fryer basket and air fry for 20 minutes, flipping the wings halfway through the cooking.
5. Meanwhile, prepare the basting sauce by combining the cayenne pepper sauce and the melted unsalted butter.
6. Using a pastry brush, baste the chicken wings with the pepper sauce.
7. Cooking for an additional 5 minutes or until the pepper sauce caramelizes.
8. Transfer the air fried chicken wings to a serving platter.

Nutritional Info (per serving):

- ✓ Calories – 385
- ✓ Fat – 30.5 g
- ✓ Fiber – 0.4 g
- ✓ Carbs – 9.8 g
- ✓ Protein – 17.5 g
- ✓ Sodium – 452 mg

Lime Chili Chicken

Prep time: 5 min + 30 min marinating| **Cooking time**: 13-15 min | **Servings** 4

This Cajun-inspired chicken dish brings in the flavor of ground cumin and combines it with the freshness of lime. What you get is a lean and mean chicken fillet that's oozing with simple yet unforgettable flavors.

If you want to lose weight or simply maintain your ideal weight, chicken breast fillet is one of the best dishes that will help reach your goal. Chicken breasts are low in fat and high in protein.

To exciting challenge lies in using the right seasonings and the correct cooking procedure. Chicken breasts grilled in the air fryer is a match made in heaven.

Ingredients:

- 4 chicken breasts, raw
- 1 lime juice
- 2 tablespoon olive oil
- ½ teaspoon ground cumin
- ½ teaspoon smoked paprika
- ¼ teaspoon cayenne pepper
- ⅛ teaspoon sea salt
- ⅛ teaspoon black pepper

Directions:

1. Pre-heat the air fryer to 350 F.
2. Combine the lime juice with the olive oil, and add in all the herbs and spices. Blend well and add to the chicken breasts. Marinate for at least 30 minutes in the refrigerator.
3. Place the marinated chicken breast fillets in the air fryer basket.
4. Grill the chicken breasts for 13 minutes or until desired doneness.
5. Transfer to a serving dish, and serve as is or topped with chopped cilantro leaves.

Nutritional Info (per serving):

- ✓ Calories – 179
- ✓ Fat – 9.6 g
- ✓ Fiber – 0.2 g
- ✓ Carbs – 1.3 g
- ✓ Protein – 21.4 g
- ✓ Sodium – 110 mg

Herbed Chicken Tenders

Prep time: 5 min | **Cooking time**: 15 min | **Servings** 4

Can't get enough of chicken? We can't blame you. Chicken is so flexible, and there are countless ways to cook it in the air fryer.

Here's one recipe you can try. This time, it's using chicken tenderloins, or chicken tenders for short.

This recipe calls for some dried herbs that are most probably in your pantry right now. Herbs, whether fresh or dried, help livens up the flavor of the chicken. Dry oregano has a stronger flavor than fresh oregano and has antioxidants.

Ingredients:

- 400 g skinless, boneless chicken tenderloins
- 1 egg
- ½ cup gluten-free panko breadcrumbs
- ¼ teaspoon dried basil
- ¼ teaspoon dried oregano
- ⅛ teaspoon salt
- ⅛ teaspoon black pepper

Directions:

1. Pre-heat the air fryer to 360 F.
2. Season with breadcrumbs with basil, oregano, salt, and pepper. Set aside.
3. Whisk the eggs in a bowl. Set aside.
4. Prepare to bread the chicken tenders. Dip each chicken tender in egg wash and then in the seasoned breadcrumbs.
5. Once breaded, transfer the chicken tenders to the basket in the air fryer. Cook for 15 minutes, flipping the chicken half into the cooking.
6. Transfer the air fried chicken tenders to a serving platter, then serve.

Nutritional Info (per serving):

- ✓ Calories – 215
- ✓ Fat – 8.5 g
- ✓ Fiber – 0.2 g
- ✓ Carbs – 2.2 g
- ✓ Protein – 30.5 g
- ✓ Sodium – 177 mg

Roasted Rosemary Chicken Thighs

Prep time: 5 min + 30 min marinating | **Cooking time**: 25 min | **Servings** 4

The beauty of air frying is its simplicity in cooking. With an air fryer, you can easily cook chicken thighs for lunch or dinner, and even throw in the side dish to cook along with it.

In this recipes, we'll roast some chicken thighs and potatoes together. This will save you time and energy so you can focus on more important things.

The bonus? You'll enjoy that roasted chicken flavor locked in, with no additional oil whatsoever. You may even remove the skin from the chicken thighs if you prefer, but the chicken skin will help keep the meat during cooking.

Ingredients:

- 400g chicken thighs, bone-in
- 1 tablespoon apple cider vinegar
- ¼ teaspoon garlic powder
- ¼ teaspoon sea salt
- ⅛ teaspoon black pepper
- ½ teaspoon dried rosemary
- 1 large potato, chopped

Directions:

1. Pre-heat the air fryer to 370 F.
2. Marinate chicken thighs in apple cider vinegar, garlic powder, sea salt, pepper and dried rosemary. Chill in the refrigerator for at least 30 minutes.
3. Place the chicken thighs in the air fryer basket and cook for 10 minutes.
4. After 10 minutes, flip the chicken pieces and cook for another 10 minutes.
5. Add the chopped potatoes and cook for 5 minutes or more, depending on your preferred doneness.
6. Transfer to serving dish, and serve.

Nutritional Info (per serving):

- ✓ Calories – 269
- ✓ Fat – 14.4 g
- ✓ Fiber – 0.1 g
- ✓ Carbs – 6.4 g
- ✓ Protein – 18.9 g
- ✓ Sodium – 349 mg

Chicken Burrito

Prep time: 5 min | **Cooking time**: 30 min | **Servings** 4

This Mexican-inspired dish is a great recommendation especially when you're always on the go, or preparing some packed meals.

As you'll see in the recipe, this calls for cooked rice, which could be a leftover from yesterday's meal. If you have brown rice, that's even better to add more fiber to your diet. But even if you don't have cooked rice to add to this recipe, it's still okay to use this recipe.

This burrito version uses chicken instead of beef, so you can cut down on the fat even more without sacrificing your protein intake.

Ingredients:

- 3 oz. boneless skinless chicken breast, diced
- 2 tablespoons extra virgin olive oil
- 1 tablespoon taco seasoning
- 1 medium bell pepper, diced
- ½ cup diced tomatoes
- 1 small onion, diced
- ½ cup leftover cooked rice
- ¼ cup tomato sauce
- 2 large gluten-free flour tortillas

Directions:

1. Pre-heat the air fryer to 360 F.
2. In a mixing bowl, combine the diced chicken breast with the taco seasoning and olive oil. Set aside.
3. In a separate bowl, combine bell peppers, onions, and tomatoes and drizzle ½ tablespoon of olive oil. Place inside the air fryer and roast for 5 minutes.
4. Add the seasoned chicken breast, and cook for 15 minutes.
5. Once the chicken is cooked, add the cooked rice and tomato sauce and mix thoroughly. Cook for another 5 minutes.
6. Remove from the air fryer and transfer to a bowl.
7. Scoop the mixture into the flour tortilla and wrap.
8. Place the wrapper burrito in the air fryer and toast for 10 minutes.
9. Transfer to a serving plate, and serve.

Nutritional Info (per serving):

- ✓ Calories – 312
- ✓ Fat – 13.3 g
- ✓ Fiber – 4.2 g
- ✓ Carbs – 25.7 g
- ✓ Protein – 21.8 g
- ✓ Sodium – 397 mg

Marinated Chicken Kebabs

Prep time: 15 min + marinating 30 min | **Cooking time**: 15-20 min | **Servings** 4

These Kebabs are easy and fun to make and turn out perfect in your Air fryer, the chicken is marinated to add a new dimension to the dish, but if preferred the chicken can be plain and seasoned with salt and pepper.

Ingredients:

- 1 large fresh Organic Chicken Breast, cut into cubes
- 16 medium sized button Mushrooms
- 1 medium Onion, cut into quarters and the layers separated
- 1 Green Capsicum cut into squares
- 8 medium Roma Tomatoes, whole
- Sea Salt and freshly cracked Black Pepper to taste
- 4 kebab skewers
- Coconut Oil as needed

For the Marinate:

- 2 tbsp of Organic Lemon Juice or half Lemon half Lime Juice
- 1 tbsp of Olive or Coconut Oil
- 1 clove of Organic Garlic, minced
- ⅛ of a tsp of Sea Salt
- ⅛ of Freshly Cracked Black Pepper

Directions:

1. Place all the ingredients in a bowl and whisk together until well combined.
2. Pour the marinade over the cubed chicken item.
3. Allow anywhere from 30 minutes to overnight for the flavor to penetrate.

To Assemble:

4. Thread a button mushroom onto the first skewer followed by a square of capsicum, add a cube of chicken, then add a slice of onion, then a tomato followed by a cube of chicken. Add another button mushroom, a square of capsicum a slice of onion and another piece of chicken. Keep adding until the skewer is filled
5. Do the other 3 skewers in the same way.
6. Spray or brush some oil onto the wire rack of your air fryer and preheat it to 360F
7. Place the kebabs on the rack in the air fryer and cook for 15 to 20 minutes
8. When finished cooking, remove the rack and draw, then allow the kebabs to rest for 3 to 5 minutes before serving.

Nutritional Info (per serving):

- ✓ Calories – 220
- ✓ Fat – 13.3 g
- ✓ Fiber – 14.2 g
- ✓ Carbs – 16.5 g
- ✓ Protein – 19.5 g
- ✓ Sodium – 287 mg

Chicken & Spinach Samosa with Cucumber Raita

Prep time: 30 min | **Cooking time**: 10 min | **Servings** 3

This traditional Indian dish is quite spicy, so for those with more western tastes use the smaller measurements of the spices specified. The cucumber Raita (a sauce or condiment that helps to temper the heat in spicy Indian dishes) adds to the enjoyment of eating this dish which can be served as a snack or part of the main meal, either hot or cold.

Ingredients for the dough:

- 2 cups of all-purpose or Vegetable Flour
- ½ a tsp of fine ground Sea Salt
- 6 tbsp of Coconut Oil or Gee
- 6 tbsp of warm Water

Ingredients the Filling:

- 1 pound of freshly ground organic Chicken
- 1 cup of cooked Chickpeas, drained
- 1 cup of finely chopped Spinach
- ½ to 2 tsp of freshly minced Green Ginger
- 2 medium-sized cloves of freshly minced Garlic
- 1 medium sized Onion, finely ground
- ½ to 2 tsp of freshly ground Cumin
- ¼ to 1 tsp of freshly ground Red Chili
- 1 to 4 tbsp of Curry Powder
- ¼ of a cup of Coconut Oil or Ghee
- Sea Salt and freshly ground Black Pepper to taste

Ingredients the Cucumber Raita:

- 2 cups of Plain Unsweetened Plain Yogurt, Dairy, Nut or Soy
- The juice of 1 medium fresh Lemon
- The Juice of 1 medium fresh Lime, juiced, the Zest may also be added.
- 1 medium English Cucumber, chopped roughly
- ½ a medium Green Chili, deseeded and chopped finely
- 1 tsp of ground Black Cumin
- 2 tsp of finely ground Sea Salt
- A dash or two of freshly ground Black Pepper

Directions for the dough:

1. Place the flour in a large bowl and add the salt and coconut oil.
2. Using your clean, dry hands, rub the oil into the flour until totally combined, the flour will look a bit like breadcrumbs.
3. Add the water and using your hands or a mixer with a bread dough hook, mix it

until all is combined and starting to turn into a firm ball. If too sticky, add a little more flour if too dry, add a small amount (1 tsp at a time) of water.

4. Place the dough on a clean surface (it is not sticky, so does not need flour dusting first) and knead it until it becomes smooth about 10 minutes.
5. Divide the dough into 6 equal sized pieces, roll them into balls and allow them to rest covered while you prepare the filling.

Directions for the Filling:

1. Place the oil or ghee in heavy bottomed saucepan on a medium to high heat
2. Add all the spices at once continually stir for about 30 seconds or until fragrant, to toast them
3. Add the onion, ginger, garlic and saute for a few minutes
4. Add the ground chicken, stirring the mixture while sauteeing, until slightly colored about 5 minutes
5. Add the cooked chickpeas and spinach, mix well and allow the mixture to simmer until the liquid is evaporated and the flavors have infused
6. Taste and season if necessary with salt and pepper
7. Place the mixture to the side and allow it to cool before filling the samosa pockets. Start making the raita.

Directions for the Cucumber Raita:

The Raita should be smooth with chunky bits of cucumber mixed in, to achieve this:

1. Place all but the cucumber in a blender or mix by hand a blend until smooth.
2. Then add the cucumber to the blender and pulse a few times to mix. If doing by hand mixing, just dice up the cucumber a bit, then mix into the Raita.

Directions to Assemble:

1. Take the balls of dough, one at a time and roll it into a circle about 1/8in thick and cut it in half to form two semicircles.
2. Form a cone, first wet all the edges with a little water, then shape the cone by folding the straightedge from the center onto its self-overlapping slightly and pinching to seal
3. Fill the cone about 2/3 fill leaving enough space to fold and seal the cone forming your samosa
4. Lightly brush the samosa with oil and repeat until all are ready to cook
5. Turn on your Air fryer and heat to 350F
6. Place all the samosa in the air fryer basket and cook for 8 to 10 minutes
7. The cooked samosa can be served hot or cold with the Cucumber Raita

Nutritional Info (per serving):

- ✓ Calories – 409
- ✓ Fat – 18.8 g
- ✓ Fiber – 5.2 g
- ✓ Carbs – 38.3 g
- ✓ Protein – 22.4 g
- ✓ Sodium – 246 mg

Air-fry Roasted Chicken

Prep time: 10 min | **Cooking time**: 1 hour | **Servings** 4

This recipe is a healthy version of rotisserie style roast chicken, seasoned with lemongrass and soy sauce.

Ingredients:

- 1 Whole Organic Chicken
- 1 to 2 tbsp of Coconut Oil or Ghee
- 2 tbsp of Organic Lemon Juice or 1 stem of Lemongrass
- 1 tbsp of Sea Salt
- 2 tbsp of Fermented Soy Sauce
- Any Seasoning you desire

Directions:

1. If the chicken has giblets, remove them and drain any liquid, then pat the outside dry.
2. Mix together the soy sauce, seasoning, and oil or ghee and rub this mixture all over the outside.
3. Fold the lemongrass and tie it together, so it fits inside the chicken body cavity.
4. Put a little salt in the chicken and insert the lemongrass inside.
5. Preheat the air fryer to 350F.
6. Oil the tray of the air fryer and place the chicken breast down in the tray.
7. Cook the chicken for 30 minutes, then flip it over and cook it for a further 30 minutes at 350F.
8. Check the internal temperature when it reaches 165F it is ready.
9. Allow the chicken to rest for 10 minutes before slicing and serving for best results.

Nutritional Info (per serving):

- ✓ Calories – 113
- ✓ Fat – 7.6 g
- ✓ Fiber – 0.1 g
- ✓ Carbs – 0.6 g
- ✓ Protein – 10.1 g
- ✓ Sodium – 293 mg

Tex-Mex Wings with Blue Cheese Dip

Prep time: 20 min + 30 min flavor infusion | Cook time: 30 min | Servings 4

Fried or BBQ chicken wings are an all-time favorite for many, especially when watching the game or meeting with the boys. Unfortunately, like many of our party snacks, they are not so good for the waistline. This recipe gives you wings that are super healthy, packed with beneficial spices, low in carbs and fats. The other good news is they are quick and easy to make and very economical.

Ingredients for the wings:

- 16 to 20 fresh organic Chicken Wings
- Ghee or Coconut Oil for basting

Ingredients for the Rub:

- 1 dried Red Chili
- 1 tsp of freshly cracked Black Pepper
- 1 tsp of crushed, dried Oregano
- 1 tsp of crushed, dried Coriander
- 1 crushed dried Bay Leaf
- ½ tsp of Black Cumin
- ½ tsp of Onion Powder
- ½ tsp of Garlic Powder
- ½ tsp of Orange Zest

Ingredients for the Dip:

- ½ cup of Sour Cream
- ½ cup of Blue Cheese, crumbled
- 1 clove of fresh, crushed Garlic
- The juice of one fresh Lime or Lemon
- 1 nip of Brandy (optional, but gives a nice tang)
- Sea Salt & Freshly Cracked Black Pepper, to taste

Directions:

1. Mix together all the rub ingredients and rub them all over and into the chicken wings.
2. Place the wings with any remaining rub into a zip-lock bag and allow them to infuse together for 30 minutes or overnight.
3. Mix together all the dip ingredients to complete the dip and place it in your refrigerator until the wings are ready.
4. When you are ready to cook the wings, preheat the air fryer to 360F and oil the cooking basket lightly.
5. Place about half the chicken wings in the basket and cook them for 10 minutes, then flip them over and cook them for another 10 minutes.
6. Cook the remaining wings in the same way.
7. When all the wings have been cooked they can all be placed in the basket and reheated for 5 minutes, then allow them to rest for another 5 minutes before serving.
8. Serve with the dip in a bowl beside the wings.

Nutritional Info (per serving):

- ✓ Calories – 199
- ✓ Fat – 13.7 g
- ✓ Fiber – 0.5 g
- ✓ Carbs – 2.9 g
- ✓ Protein – 15.3 g
- ✓ Sodium – 276 mg

Air Fryer Beef & Pork Recipes

Roasted Boneless Pork Chop

Prep time: 5 min | **Cooking time**: 20 min | **Servings** 4

This classic pork chop recipe gets an upgrade with a little oyster sauce. This dark and savory liquid is a flavor enhancer and provides you sodium for your diet.

Remember, the key to a healthy lifestyle is to nourish your body with a variety of nutrients in moderation. That includes sodium, as well as other nutrients. Sodium is needed by our body in enzyme operations, as well as in muscle health.

Balance and portion control should be well incorporated in your meal planning. So for this recipe, just the right amount of oyster sauce is added to impart that umami flavor to your pork chops.

Ingredients:

- 500g boneless skinless pork chops, raw
- 1 teaspoon oyster sauce
- ½ lemon (juice)
- 2 teaspoons olive oil
- ⅛ teaspoon black pepper

Directions:

1. Pre-heat the air fryer to 360 F.
2. Season the pork chops in oyster sauce, lemon juice, olive oil and black pepper.
3. Place the pork chops into the air fryer basket and cook for 20 minutes.
4. Serve.

Nutritional Info (per serving):

- ✓ Calories – 269
- ✓ Fat – 20.2 g
- ✓ Fiber – 0.2 g
- ✓ Carbs – 1.2 g
- ✓ Protein – 21.3 g
- ✓ Sodium – 284 mg

Garlic Beef Steak

Prep time: 5 min + 30 min marinating | **Cooking time**: 6-10 min | **Servings** 4

Here's another steak recipe you can do in a snap: Garlic Beef Steak. Finally, you impress someone with your steak cooking abilities using the trusty air fryer.

Learn this recipe and master how to prepare perfectly cooked steaks. The air fryer is easy to use so you'll be an expert in no time.

Ingredients:

- 400g lean beef flank, raw
- 1 tablespoon olive oil
- 1 tablespoon cider vinegar
- 1 tablespoon Worcestershire sauce
- 1 tablespoon light soy sauce
- ½ teaspoon garlic powder
- ¼ teaspoon onion powder
- ⅛ teaspoon black pepper
- 1 tablespoon mustard

Directions:

1. Pre-heat the air fryer to 350 F.
2. In a container with cover, prepare the marinade by combining the olive oil, balsamic vinegar, Worcestershire sauce, soy sauce, garlic, onion powder, white pepper and mustard.
3. Add the steaks into the marinade and coat well.
4. Cover the container and let the steaks marinate inside the refrigerator for at least 30 minutes.
5. Once marinated for at least 30 minutes, place the steaks inside the cooking basket.
6. Cook for around 8 to 10 minutes for a well done steak. If you prefer a medium rare steak, decrease cooking down to 6 -7 minutes only.
7. Once cooked to your preferred doneness, transfer to a serving dish.
8. Serve.

Nutritional Info (per serving):

- ✓ Calories – 227
- ✓ Fat – 13.3 g
- ✓ Fiber – 0.5 g
- ✓ Carbs – 2.2 g
- ✓ Protein – 23.3 g
- ✓ Sodium – 272 mg

Easy Pork Ribs

Prep time: 5 min + 30 min marinating | **Cooking time**: 30 min | **Servings** 2

Just the mere mention of ribs and you can probably imagine fall-off-the-bone type of meals. Well, here's a variation of that imagery.

Why don't we make a simple and easy rib dish that's done in an hour? Yes, with an air fryer you can do that.

The air fryer's technology allows you to roast ribs and make them tender while locking in the flavors.

Ingredients:

- 500g pork ribs, raw
- ½ teaspoon garlic powder
- ¼ teaspoon black pepper
- ½ teaspoon salt
- 1 teaspoon Worcestershire sauce

Directions:

1. Pre-heat the air fryer to 350 F.
2. Wash the pork ribs and cut into serving sizes.
3. Add the garlic powder, salt, pepper and Worcestershire sauce to the pork ribs and mix thoroughly.
4. Marinate in the refrigerator for at least 30 minutes.
5. Place the pork ribs into the air fryer and roast for 15 minutes.
6. Pull out the basket and turn the pork ribs. Cook for another 15 minutes.
7. Serve.

Nutritional Info (per serving):

- ✓ Calories – 235
- ✓ Fat – 14.4 g
- ✓ Fiber – 0.1 g
- ✓ Carbs – 0.6 g
- ✓ Protein – 24.4 g
- ✓ Sodium – 382 mg

Classic Sirloin Steak Recipe

Prep time: 5 min | **Cooking time**: 10-15 min | **Servings** 2

Properly cooked beef steak is simply a must for those special meals once in a while. Yes, you can have this on any regular day of the week. After all, cooking steaks in an air fryer is a breeze that you need not wait for weekend to prepare something special.

In this recipe, we stick to simple seasonings to enhance the flavor of beef. A classic steak doesn't need anything else other than the basic salt and pepper combo. You know what makes a good steak really awesome? It's the proper mix of time and temperature. With an air fryer, you can do that. Keep practicing and explore an entirely new way of making steaks.

Ingredients:

- 400g sirloin steak, raw
- 1 teaspoon olive oil
- ¼ teaspoon salt
- ¼ teaspoon black pepper

Directions:

1. Pre-heat the air fryer to 400 F.
2. Season the steak with salt and pepper on both sides and rub with olive oil.
3. Place the steak in the air fryer and cook for 5 minutes.
4. Flip the steak and cook for another 4-5 minutes for medium rare.
5. If you prefer a medium well to well done steak, cook for a total of 12-14 minutes flipping it in between.
6. Remove from the air fryer and let it rest for about 10 minutes before slicing.
7. Serve.

Nutritional Info (per serving):

- ✓ Calories – 291
- ✓ Fat – 10.3 g
- ✓ Fiber – 0.1 g
- ✓ Carbs – 0.2 g
- ✓ Protein – 46 g
- ✓ Sodium – 291 mg

Air Fried Beef Patties

Prep time: 10 min | **Cooking time**: 10-15 min | **Servings** 4

Gone are the days when beef patties are only meant to be cooked outside on the grill. While that's an amazing way to cook beef patties, sometimes you long for something simpler. Well, that's why the air fryer was invented.

It can tackle almost anything from air frying French fries to grilling beef patties. Now if you miss that smokiness, here's what you can do. Throw in a few drops of liquid smoke to this recipe, and you're good to go.

If not, let's do simple air fried (or you can say air-grilled) beef patties using the recipe below. Make sure to use lean ground beef to really keep the fat to a minimum.

Ingredients:

- 500g 85% lean ground beef
- ½ teaspoon garlic powder
- ½ teaspoon onion powder
- ¼ teaspoon black pepper
- ¼ teaspoon salt

Directions:

1. Pre-heat the air fryer to 350 F.
2. Combine the ground beef together with the seasonings: garlic powder, onion powder, salt and black pepper.
3. Form the seasoned ground beef into 4 patties.
4. Grill the beef patties in the air fryer for 10 minutes for medium doneness. If you prefer a well-done patty, cook for 3-5 more minutes.
5. Transfer to a serving platter. Serve on a bun or with some side noodles. (Optional)

Nutritional Info (per serving):

- ✓ Calories – 312
- ✓ Fat – 18.8 g
- ✓ Fiber – 0.1 g
- ✓ Carbs – 0.6 g
- ✓ Protein – 32.2 g
- ✓ Sodium – 236 mg

Pork Tenderloin

Prep time: 5 + 15 min marinating | **Cooking time**: 15 min | **Servings** 2

Here's another pork dish we recommend for one of your dinners. For this recipe, we'll enhance the flavor of pork with dried oregano and mustard.

As a condiment, mustard plays an important role in nutrition since mustard seeds are high in selenium and magnesium. Both of them are anti-inflammatory so your body needs a healthy dose of these compounds. Mustard not only flavors your food but also nourishes your body.

Cook this pork tenderloin easily with an air fryer. It's best to marinate the meat for a longer time, but if you're in a hurry, feel free to cut down marinating time even for just 15 minutes.

Ingredients:

- 500 g boneless pork loin, raw
- 1 tablespoon olive oil
- 2 teaspoon mustard
- ½ teaspoon dried oregano
- ¼ teaspoon black pepper

Directions:

1. Pre-heat the air fryer to 400 F.
2. Cut the pork loin into 4 pieces.
3. Rub the meat with olive oil, mustard, oregano, salt, and pepper.
4. Place the pork loin in the air fryer basket and cook for 15 minutes, turning the meat over halfway within the cooking time.
5. Transfer to a serving dish.
6. Serve with a salad or a starch of your choice.

Nutritional Info (per serving):

- ✓ Calories – 167
- ✓ Fat – 7.0 g
- ✓ Fiber – 0.2 g
- ✓ Carbs – 1.4 g
- ✓ Protein – 23.6 g
- ✓ Sodium – 274 mg

Sweet & Sour Pork

Prep time: 10 min | **Cooking time**: 10 min | **Servings** 2

This Chinese-inspired dish is great for a quick weekday dinner, instead of just ordering the usual Chinese takeout.

With an air fryer, you'll look forward to cooking at home as it makes cooking so much easier.

Use a boneless pork loin for this recipe, but any lean cut of pork will do. The important thing is to cut it the same size to cook them uniformly in the air fryer. We'll add some fresh pineapples and bell peppers to the pork, making this dish quite refreshing. The citrus notes will balance the savory taste of pork. And add zing to life!

Ingredients:

- 500 g boneless pork loin, cut into 1-inch cubes, raw
- ¼ teaspoon salt
- ⅛ teaspoon black pepper
- ¼ teaspoon ginger powder
- ½ cup potato starch
- ½ cup fresh pineapples, cut into 1-inch cubes
- ½ cup red or green bell pepper, roughly chopped
- 1 medium stalk celery, cut into 2-inch stalks

Directions:

1. Pre-heat the air fryer to 360 F.
2. Season the pork with salt, black pepper and ginger powder.
3. Dredge the seasoned pork with potato starch.
4. Add the pork cubes in the air fryer and cook for 7 minutes.
5. Shake the basket to flip the pork pieces. Add the pineapples, bell pepper and celery. Cook for 3 minutes.
6. Transfer the pork and sidings to a mixing bowl and toss in sweet and sour sauce.
7. Serve over a bowl of rice, or on a serving dish.

Nutritional Info (per serving):

- ✓ Calories – 438
- ✓ Fat – 20.2 g
- ✓ Fiber – 0.8 g
- ✓ Carbs – 37.1 g
- ✓ Protein – 25.3 g
- ✓ Sodium – 436 mg

Beef Meatballs

Prep time: 5 min | **Cooking time**: 7-8 min | **Servings** 4

Meatballs are so versatile you can create a lot of dishes with these cute little balls.

Here's a simple recipe to try for beef meatballs. Beef provides your body nutrients like protein, iron, zinc, and a lot of the B vitamins too. Did you know that half of the fat in beef in actually monounsaturated? In other words, it's a healthy kind of fat that's good your heart.

We'll combine these meatballs with a bowlful of salad greens to make this dish even healthier.

Ingredients:

- 400 g beef mince, lean
- ½ teaspoon ground dried oregano
- ½ teaspoon ground dried thyme
- ½ teaspoon garlic powder
- ½ teaspoon onion powder
- ¼ teaspoon salt
- ⅛ teaspoon black pepper
- ¼ cup (approximately 25 g) bread crumbs
- 1 egg
- 4 cups mixed baby greens or any salad green of your choice

Directions:

1. Pre-heat the air fryer to 400 F.
2. In a mixing bowl, combine the minced beef with the oregano, thyme, garlic powder, onion powder, salt, black pepper.
3. Add the bread crumbs and eggs and mix thoroughly.
4. Shape the beef mixture into 16 balls.
5. Place the meatballs in the air fryer and cook for 7-8 minutes or until brown.
6. Transfer the cooked meatballs to a mixing boss and toss with some teriyaki sauce (optional).
7. Place the meatballs over some salad greens. Serve.

Nutritional Info (per serving):

- ✓ Calories – 162
- ✓ Fat – 5.1 g
- ✓ Fiber – 0.2 g
- ✓ Carbs – 5.8 g
- ✓ Protein – 23.5 g
- ✓ Sodium – 191 mg

Pork in Yogurt Bites

Prep time: 5 min + 30 min marinating | **Cooking time**: 10-12 min | **Servings** 4

This Indian-inspired pork dish is made with lean pork to minimize fat content. The meat is marinated in fat-free yogurt to keep it moist while air frying.

A combination of spices (ginger, cumin, coriander, and turmeric) makes this dish extra flavorful without the extra calories.

To balance the taste, pair with some starch of your choice, like whole wheat fusilli or some steamed brown rice.

Ingredients:

- 20 oz. lean pork, cubed
- ½ cup light yogurt, fat-free
- ½ tsp ginger powder
- ½ tsp ground cumin
- ¼ tsp ground coriander
- ¼ tsp ground turmeric
- ⅛ tsp salt
- ⅛ tsp black pepper
- Sprigs of basil for garnish

Directions:

1. Pre-heat the air fryer to 400 F.
2. In a mixing bowl, combine the pork cubes with yogurt, ginger powder, cumin, coriander, turmeric, salt, and black pepper.
3. Marinate in the refrigerator for at least 30 minutes.
4. Place the marinated pork cubes in a baking dish and air fry for 10-12 minutes or until pork is fully cooked.
5. Transfer to the serving plate and serve with the starch of your choice. Garnish with sprigs of basil and serve.

Nutritional Info (per serving):

- ✓ Calories – 240
- ✓ Fat – 5.6 g
- ✓ Fiber – 0.1 g
- ✓ Carbs – 5.1 g
- ✓ Protein – 40.5 g
- ✓ Sodium – 95 mg

Homemade Meatloaf

Prep time: 10 min | **Cooking time**: 25 min | **Servings** 4

Meatloaf is comfort food for many. It's easy to prepare as it's one of that mix and bake type of dishes. Here's a healthy take on the classic meatloaf which you can easily create using your air fryer. Use lean minced meat eat to keep those fats at bay. We used lean beef mince in this recipe, but feel free to use lean pork mince if you like.

This protein-packed dish can be a great weekday dinner after work or be hitting the gym. Just pop in the air fryer and bake. Why you can even take a shower while it bakes in the air fryer! What can be more convenient than that?

Ingredients:

- 16 oz. beef mince, lean
- 4 tbsp. gluten-free breadcrumbs
- 1 tbsp. olive oil
- 2 tbsp. reduced fat milk
- ½ cup green beans, raw, trimmed & diced
- 1 medium carrot, shredded
- ¼ tsp onion powder
- ¼ tsp dried thyme
- ⅛ tsp black pepper

Directions:

1. Pre-heat the air fryer to 390 F.
2. In a mixing bowl, combine beef mince with all the ingredients and blend together until well mixed.
3. Pour the beef mixture into a meatloaf pan and place inside the air fryer.
4. Bake the meatloaf for 25 minutes or until the meat is done.
5. Remove from the air fryer and let cool for 10 minutes before slicing.
6. Transfer to a serving dish, and serve with additional vegetables if preferred.

Nutritional Info (per serving):

- ✓ Calories – 201
- ✓ Fat – 9.4 g
- ✓ Fiber – 0.9 g
- ✓ Carbs – 4.6 g
- ✓ Protein – 24.7 g
- ✓ Sodium – 24 mg

Air Stir Fry Beef with Carrots and Spinach

Prep time: 5 min + 30 min marinating| **Cooking time**: 12 min | **Servings** 4

Instead of stir-frying beef, we'll air fry them at a high temperature. The intense heat will lock in the meat juices to keep them moist and tender. In this recipe, we'll use beef sirloin, but you can also use other cuts tender cuts of beef such as ranch, flank or skirt steak. To add vitamins and minerals to this protein-rich dish, we'll throw in some carrots and spinach. Cook them very briefly to preserve the nutrients.

Ingredients:

- 400 g lean beef sirloin steak, raw, thinly sliced
- ½ cup organic apple cider vinegar, raw unfiltered
- 1 tbsp. cornstarch, all natural
- 2 tsp pure sesame oil
- 2 cup spinach leaves, blanched
- 1 tbsp. oyster sauce
- ¼ tsp ginger ground
- ¼ tsp onion powder
- ⅛ tsp black pepper
- 1 medium carrot, sliced

Directions:

1. Pre-heat the air fryer to 400 F.
2. In a mixing bowl, combine the beef with apple cider vinegar, cornstarch, sesame oil, oyster sauce, ground ginger, onion powder, and black pepper. Mix well until cornstarch is evenly blended.
3. Marinate the beef in the refrigerator for at least 30 minutes.
4. Place the marinated beef on a baking dish and cook in the air fryer for 10 minutes.
5. Stir the beef, then add the carrots and spinach on top of the beef and cook for an additional 2 minutes.
6. Transfer cooked beef and vegetables to a serving dish and serve.

Nutritional Info (per serving):

- ✓ Calories – 201
- ✓ Fat – 8.8 g
- ✓ Fiber – 0.7 g
- ✓ Carbs – 5.3 g
- ✓ Protein – 23.6 g
- ✓ Sodium – 205 mg

Beef with Pepper and Mushrooms

Prep time: 5 min | **Cooking time**: 12 min | **Servings** 4

Here's another quick beef dish that's guaranteed to nourish you well. Bell peppers are known for their nutritional benefits, as well as adding crunch and sweetness to a dish.

In this recipe, we'll use red bell pepper since this variety provides the highest amount of vitamin C in bell pepper. Aside from their infection-fighting property, bell peppers also have phytochemicals and beta-carotene that act as antioxidants.

If possible, use grass-fed beef. Compared to other types of beef, grass-fed beef may have less total fat and more omega-3 fatty acids. Plus, it has a good type of fat to help improve heart health.

Ingredients:

- 400 g grass-fed beef, sirloin fillet
- 2 medium red bell pepper, chopped
- 1 cup mushrooms, raw pieces
- 2 tbsp. olive oil
- 2 tbsp. balsamic vinegar
- ⅛ tsp salt
- ⅛ tsp black pepper

Directions:

1. Pre-heat the air fryer to 400 F.
2. In a mixing bowl, season the beef with salt and black pepper.
3. Place the beef in a baking dish, along with the chopped bell peppers and cut mushrooms. Drizzle with olive oil and balsamic vinegar.
4. Cook in the air fryer for 12 minutes or until the beef is done.
5. Transfer the cooked beef and vegetables to a serving dish.

Nutritional Info (per serving):

- ✓ Calories – 185
- ✓ Fat – 9.8 g
- ✓ Fiber – 1.2 g
- ✓ Carbs – 5.0 g
- ✓ Protein – 24.1 g
- ✓ Sodium – 150 mg

Grilled Pork Chop and Kale Chips

Prep time: 5 min | **Cooking time**: 20-23 min | **Servings** 4

In this recipe, we're pairing air fried pork with a superstar vegetable – the kale!

Kale is part of the cruciferous vegetable family known for their cancer-fighting property. They're rich in glucosinolates which are anti-inflammatory, antibacterial and antiviral.

Because of this goodness, kale has achieved enormous popularity, and it's high time for you to include it regularly in your diet.

Ingredients:

- 4 pcs pork chops, bone-in, skinless
- ¼ tsp ground sage
- 4 servings kale, raw, ribs removed
- ⅛ tsp salt
- ⅛ tsp black pepper
- 1 tbsp. olive oil

Directions:

1. Pre-heat the air fryer to 360 F.
2. Season the pork chops with sage, salt, and black pepper.
3. In a separate bowl, toss the kale in olive oil.
4. Place the pork chops in the air fryer and cook for 18 minutes.
5. Open the air fryer basket and add the kale over the pork chops. Close the basket and cook for 2-5 minutes more or until kale is crispy.
6. Transfer air fried pork and kale to a serving platter. Serve with an optional applesauce on the side.

Nutritional Info (per serving):

- ✓ Calories – 273
- ✓ Fat – 17.3 g
- ✓ Fiber – 1.3 g
- ✓ Carbs – 9.9 g
- ✓ Protein – 21.9 g
- ✓ Sodium – 111 mg

Pork Ribs

Prep time: 5 min+ 30 min marinating | **Cooking time**: 15 min | **Servings** 4

Pork ribs are quite adaptable. You can have them for picnics, or even on a fancy dinner with some wine. However you want your ribs, this recipe will not make you feel guilty at all.

With an air fryer and carefully selected ingredients, this dish is low in sodium which providing you enough protein for muscle building.

Add these ribs to some salad greens, and you'll have a nice dinner ready in just a few minutes. Don't forget that glass of wine!

Ingredients:

- 400 g pork ribs, raw and cut into serving pieces
- ¼ cup olive oil
- 1 tbsp. reduced sodium Worcestershire sauce
- ¼ cup low sodium soy sauce
- 2 tbsp. low sodium ketchup
- ⅛ tsp black pepper

Directions:

1. Pre-heat the air fryer to 400 F.
2. Marinate the pork ribs in olive oil, soy sauce, ketchup, Worcestershire and black pepper for at least 30 minutes in the refrigerator.
3. Place the marinated ribs on a baking pan and fry for 15 minutes.
4. Transfer the cooked ribs to a serving platter, and serve with an optional mixed greens salad.

Nutritional Info (per serving):

- ✓ Calories – 297
- ✓ Fat – 23 g
- ✓ Fiber – 0.0 g
- ✓ Carbs – 3.7 g
- ✓ Protein – 18.1 g
- ✓ Sodium – 64 mg

Beef Goulash

Prep time: 5 min | **Cooking time**: 30 min | **Servings** 4

For this beef recipe, we'll use the beef cut for stews, but you can use other cuts good for braising such as beef chuck or brisket.

This saucy dish will be a good pairing for some starch – whether whole wheat pasta or some brown rice. We added some sweet red peppers aside from the main spice which is Hungarian paprika, so expect this dish to explode with flavors.

If you don't have Hungarian paprika, regular smoked paprika will do.

Ingredients:

- 400 g beef stew meat, cut into 1-inch cubes
- 1 medium onion, diced
- ½ tsp paprika, Hungarian
- 1 cup chopped sweet red pepper
- 2 large tomatoes, chopped
- 1 bay leaf
- ⅛ tsp salt
- ⅛ tsp black pepper
- 2 cups of water

Directions:

1. Pre-heat the air fryer to 400 F.
2. In a baking pan, place the diced onion and cook for 3-5 minutes or just until they start to caramelize.
3. Pull out the air fryer basket, then add the paprika and beef to the onions and mix well. Return the air fryer basket and cook for 7 minutes or until the beef is no longer red.
4. Add the sweet red peppers and cook for 5 minutes.
5. Add water, tomatoes, bay leaf, salt, and black pepper to the beef mixture. Reduce the temperature to 350 F and cook for 10-15 minutes or until the sauce thickens. Check every 5 minutes to make sure the sauce does not dry up.
6. Once the sauce has thickened, remove from the air fryer.
7. Transfer to a serving bowl. Add some cooked pasta (optional) then serve.

Nutritional Info (per serving):

- ✓ Calories – 181
- ✓ Fat – 6.0 g
- ✓ Fiber – 2.2 g
- ✓ Carbs – 8.9 g
- ✓ Protein – 23.6 g
- ✓ Sodium – 138 mg

Pork Schnitzel in Mushroom Sauce

Prep time: 5 min | **Cooking time**: 30 min | **Servings** 4

This lean pork recipe calls for thin slices of meat, which will be beautifully embraced by the mushroom sauce.

To balance the nutrients as this is already rich in protein, add some side salad for vitamins and minerals, and starch for carbohydrates. Flavor-wise, the mushrooms will add a depth of earthy flavors to the dish.

We use button mushrooms but feel free to use other types of mushrooms that may be available to you. What's important is that they are roasted well in the air fryer to bring out their flavors.

Ingredients:

- 400g lean pork, raw, cut into thin slices
- 1 cup button mushrooms, raw pieces
- 2 tbsp. all-purpose flour
- 2 tbsp. olive oil
- ½ tsp dried thyme
- ¼ tsp salt
- ¼ tsp black pepper
- 1 cup of water

Directions:

1. Pre-heat the air fryer to 390 F.
2. Season the pork with salt and black pepper.
3. Place the pork in the air fryer basket and cook for 10-12 minutes or until pork is done.
4. Transfer the cooked pork to a serving platter.
5. Prepare the mushroom gravy. Place the mushrooms on a baking pan and drizzle with olive oil. Cook in the air fryer for about 5 minutes.
6. Add the flour and mix well into the mushrooms. Add water, thyme, salt, and black pepper. Reduce heat to 350 F and cook for 10-13 minutes or until sauce thickens.
7. Once the gravy has thickened, remove from the air fryer.
8. Pour the mushroom gravy over the pork, then serve.

Nutritional Info (per serving):

- ✓ Calories – 219
- ✓ Fat – 11.1 g
- ✓ Fiber – 0.3 g
- ✓ Carbs – 1.5 g
- ✓ Protein – 28.7 g
- ✓ Sodium – 148 mg

Minced Pork with Fresh Coriander

Prep time: 5 min | **Cooking time**: 15 min | **Servings** 4

This minced pork recipe has an Oriental flair to it and adds variety to your everyday meals. Use lean pork mince as much as possible.

Aside from boosting the nutrients, we add some fresh coriander and ginger to provide a flavor contrast with the pork. Coriander is a wonderful herb that provides dietary fiber, as well as manganese, magnesium, iron, vitamin C, and vitamin K. Ginger, on the other hand, helps balance blood sugar.

To further season this dish, we add a touch of fish sauce towards the end of cooking.

Ingredients:

- 400 g pork mince, lean
- 1 tsp sesame oil
- 10g fresh ginger, minced
- ½ cup fresh coriander, chopped
- ¼ tsp chili powder
- ½ tsp garlic powder
- ⅛ tsp black pepper
- 1 tsp fish sauce

Directions:

1. Pre-heat the air fryer to 400 F.
2. In a baking pan, season the pork mince with sesame oil, fresh ginger, chili powder, garlic powder, and black pepper.
3. Place inside air fryer basket and cook for 8-10 minutes or until the pork is light brown.
4. Add ½ cup water, fish sauce, and chopped coriander to the pork mixture. Mix well and cook further for 5 minutes.
5. Remove from the air fryer and transfer to a serving dish.

Nutritional Info (per serving):

- ✓ Calories – 133
- ✓ Fat – 4.7 g
- ✓ Fiber – 0.2 g
- ✓ Carbs – 0.7 g
- ✓ Protein – 21.2 g
- ✓ Sodium – 160 mg

Air Fried Pork with Ketchup

Prep time: 5 min | **Cooking time**: 12-15 min | **Servings** 4

Here's another simple pork dish that can be served either as an appetizer or main dish. Adding ketchup makes it almost like party food. With the texture that is produced by cooking this in the air fryer, this is really one fun, crunchy dish.

If you're hosting a small dinner party, this is the perfect chit-chat food. You may have to cut the pork pieces even smaller if you're serving them as hors-d'oeuvres.

As always, use lean cuts of meat to minimize the fat content. Doing this little step in choosing well your ingredients is one key step in losing weight.

Ingredients:

- 450 g lean pork, cut into 1.5-inch pieces
- ¼ cup cornstarch
- ⅛ tsp salt
- ⅛ tsp black pepper
- ¼ cup low sodium ketchup
- ¼ tsp cayenne pepper
- 2 tbsp. olive oil

Directions:

1. Pre-heat the air fryer to 400 F.
2. In a mixing bowl, toss the pork with cornstarch, salt, and black pepper.
3. Place in the air fryer and cook for 10-12 minutes or until pork starts to turn brown and crunchy. Shake the air fryer basket hallway in the cooking to flip the pork pieces.
4. Add the ketchup, cayenne pepper, and olive oil to the pork, and mix until pork is well coated. Cook for another 2-3 minutes or until pork is well cooked.
5. Transfer the air fried pork to a serving platter and serve with an optional fresh parsley garnish.

Nutritional Info (per serving):

- ✓ Calories – 257
- ✓ Fat – 11.1 g
- ✓ Fiber – 0.2 g
- ✓ Carbs – 11.2 g
- ✓ Protein – 28.3 g
- ✓ Sodium – 77 mg

Air Fryer Fish & Seafood Recipes

Spicy Coconut Macadamia Catfish

Prep time: 15 min | **Cooking time**: 15 min | **Servings** 4

In the mood for something spicy? Try this dish inspired by the island life, with healthy fats from buttery macadamia nuts and wheat-free, high-fiber coconut flour. The cayenne pepper adds zing to the dish, making this a good pairing for some fresh salads to balance the heat.

Ingredients:

- 4-6-oz catfish fillets
- 1 piece egg
- ½ cup of coconut flour
- ¼ cup chopped macadamia nuts
- ¼ tsp of cayenne pepper
- ¼ tsp of paprika
- ½ tsp of garlic powder
- ½ tsp sea salt
- ⅛ tsp black pepper

Directions:

1. Combine the egg, water, coconut flour, chopped macadamia nuts, cayenne pepper, paprika, garlic powder, sea salt and black pepper to create a thick batter.
2. Dip each of the fillets into the batter mixture until evenly coated.
3. Place the catfish fillets in the basket/tray.
4. Cook in the air fryer at 375 F for 15 minutes or until golden brown.
5. Remove the fish and plate with some mint leaves and chili peppers as a garnish before serving.

Nutritional Info (per serving):

- ✓ Calories – 478
- ✓ Fat – 25.8 g
- ✓ Fiber – 1.7 g
- ✓ Carbs – 3.0 g
- ✓ Protein – 53.5 g
- ✓ Sodium – 375 mg

Quick & Easy Crispy Lemon Cod

Prep time: 5 min + 30 min marinating | **Cooking time**: 15 min | **Servings** 4

This fish recipe is so simple and quick to prepare yet bursting with flavor. Marinating it in vitamin and mineral packed lemon juice makes this a healthy option for a light lunch or dinner. Cod is a good source of omega-3 fatty acids so this dish is truly heart-friendly. Plus, it's rich in vitamin B12 and a great non-meat protein-source.

Ingredients:

- 4 piece cod fillets
- Juice of 1 piece lemon
- 1 tsp lemon zest
- ½ tsp sea salt
- ¼ tsp black pepper
- 4 pieces cherry tomatoes
- 1 serving of mashed potatoes
- 1 arugula leaf

Directions:

1. Place cod fillets in a shallow pan.
2. Season both sides of the fillets with sea salt and pepper.
3. Add the lemon juice and lemon zest over the fillets.
4. Chill in the refrigerator for at least 30 minutes.
5. Place the marinated cod fillets in the basket/tray.
6. Cook in the air fryer at 375 F for 15 minutes or until golden brown.
7. Remove the fish and plate with some halved cherry tomatoes, mashed potatoes and arugula before serving.

Nutritional Info (per serving):

- ✓ Calories – 148
- ✓ Fat – 1.8 g
- ✓ Fiber – 0.4 g
- ✓ Carbs – 11.8 g
- ✓ Protein – 21.7 g
- ✓ Sodium – 443 mg

Corn Flakes Crusted White Swai

Prep time: 15 min | **Cooking time**: 5 min | **Servings** 4

The beauty of this dish lies in textural crunch from the corn flakes complementing the flaky tenderness of the white swai. Should you prefer a different kind of fish, this recipe will work just as fine. You can have a sablefish or black cod, or some albacore tuna.

Ingredients:

- 12-oz white swai fillets
- 1 cup corn flakes, crushed
- ¼ tsp garlic powder
- ½ tsp sea salt
- ¼ tsp black pepper
- 1 tsp extra-virgin olive oil

Directions:

1. Preheat the air fryer at 375 F for about 5 minutes.
2. Combine and mix together the crushed corn flakes, garlic powder, sea salt, pepper and extra-virgin olive oil.
3. Spread the corn flakes mixture on a platter.
4. Coat each white swai fillet by laying it over the corn flakes mixture and pressing it lightly until the mixture sticks to the fish. Do the same for the other side.
5. Place the breaded white swai in the basket/tray in a single layer.
6. Cook in the air fryer at 375 F for 5 minutes or until golden brown.
7. Remove the fish and plate with some halved cherry tomatoes, mashed potatoes and arugula before serving.

Nutritional Info (per serving):

- ✓ Calories – 116
- ✓ Fat – 3.7 g
- ✓ Fiber – 0.4 g
- ✓ Carbs – 6.3 g
- ✓ Protein – 15.5 g
- ✓ Sodium – 215 mg

Light Beer-Battered Fish & Chips

Prep time: 15 min | **Cooking time**: 10-15 min | **Servings** 3

Here's a recipe to try on a Friday night or perhaps over the weekend. It's the perfect bar chow that's easy to prepare with an air fryer on hand. Use a low-carb light beer to avoid adding calories, but still adding some flavor. Instead of wheat flour for the batter, almond flour/meal is used, which is gluten-free, high in protein and fiber, and low in carbohydrate. For the fries, go for the sweet potatoes.

Ingredients:

- 12-oz haddock fillets
- 2 cups almond flour/meal
- 1 12-oz-bottle light beer
- ¼ tsp sea salt
- ¼ tsp paprika
- ½ tsp crushed red pepper flakes
- ⅛ tsp black pepper

Directions:

1. Preheat the air fryer to 350 F for about 5 minutes.
2. In a shallow bowl, combine half of the almond meal, paprika, red pepper flakes, and black pepper. Set aside.
3. Combine the beer with sea salt and the rest of the almond meal in a bowl and whisk together until free from lumps.
4. Coat the fish with the dry almond meal mixture and shake off the excess.
5. Dip the coated fish in the beer batter.
6. Place the battered fish in the tray in a single layer.
7. Cook in the air fryer at 350 F for 10-15 minutes or until golden brown.
8. Serve immediately with air fried sweet potato fries.

Nutritional Info (per serving):

- ✓ Calories – 197
- ✓ Fat – 8.1 g
- ✓ Fiber – 1.6 g
- ✓ Carbs – 4.7 g
- ✓ Protein – 23.3 g
- ✓ Sodium – 485 mg

Parmesan-Crusted Tilapia Fillet

Prep time: 15 min | **Cooking time**: 10-12 min | **Servings** 4

Another quick and easy fish recipe that's' perfect for a light lunch with a salad, or some organic brown rice. Using parmesan as a breading instead of the usual wheat flour reduces the carbohydrates in this dish. It gives a nice, crusty texture to your fish fillet, and that parmesan flavor will surely delight any cheese lover.

Ingredients:

- 12-ozs tilapia fillets
- ¼ cup shredded parmesan
- 1 tsp paprika
- ¼ tsp black pepper
- ¼ cup extra-virgin olive oil

Directions:

1. Preheat the air fryer to 375 F for about 5 minutes.
2. Combine parmesan, paprika, and black pepper in a shallow platter.
3. Coat the tilapia fillets with olive oil.
4. Press both sides of the coated tilapia fillets into the parmesan mixture until the cheese sticks to the fish.
5. Place the crusted fish in the tray in a single layer.
6. Cook in the air fryer at 375 F for 10-12 minutes or until golden brown.
7. Serve immediately with air fried sweet potato fries.

Nutritional Info (per serving):

- ✓ Calories – 410
- ✓ Fat – 17.1 g
- ✓ Fiber – 0.2 g
- ✓ Carbs – 0.5 g
- ✓ Protein – 65.0 g
- ✓ Sodium – 205 mg

Roasted Prawns

Prep time: 5 min | **Cooking time**: 15 min | **Servings** 4

Prawns are easy to cook and shouldn't take too long especially in an air fryer. Just season the prawns and let the air fryer do its magic.

This recipe uses simple ingredients and seasoning to preserve the flavor of the prawns and not mask it. The juice from the lime will provide freshness to the dish, while the parsley will add some herbal flavors.

Ingredients:

- 4 packs jumbo king prawns, raw (120g per pack)
- 2 garlic cloves, minced
- 1 lime, juice
- ¼ cup olive oil
- ¼ cup parsley
- ¼ tsp salt
- ⅛ tsp black pepper

Directions:

1. Preheat the air fryer to 390 F.
2. Place the cleaned prawns in a baking dish and season with garlic, lime juice, olive oil, parsley, salt, and black pepper.
3. Place in air fryer and roast for 15 minutes or until the prawns have turned pink and just cooked through.
4. Transfer to serving dish and serve with additional parsley leaves as garnish.

Nutritional Info (per serving):

- ✓ Calories – 262
- ✓ Fat – 13.9 g
- ✓ Fiber – 1.2 g
- ✓ Carbs – 3.2 g
- ✓ Protein – 32.1 g
- ✓ Sodium – 350 mg

Crispy Breaded Shrimps

Prep time: 10 min | **Cooking time**: 8 min | **Servings** 4

If you're looking for a seafood recipe that can be an appetizer for your next party, this is it. Not only is this recipe easy to prepare but also a feast for the eyes, making it an easy conversation topic on your party.

But if you're not throwing a party and you just want some crunchy dishes to add to your usual dinner, this recipe will work just as well. Don't forget to use shrimps with tail-on as it's essential for visual presentation. It also serves as a nice little handle if you're serving this as finger food.

Ingredients:

- 500g raw shrimps, peeled, tail-on
- ½ cup all-purpose flour
- 1 egg, beaten
- ¾ cup panko breadcrumbs
- ½ tsp smoked paprika
- ¼ tsp salt
- ⅛ tsp black pepper

Directions:

1. Preheat the air fryer to 400 F.
2. Combine the cleaned shrimps with smoked paprika, salt, and black pepper to season.
3. Prepare to bread the shrimps by dipping each one in flour, then egg, then breadcrumbs.
4. Add the breaded shrimps to the air fryer basket and air fry for 8 minutes, flipping the shrimps halfway in the cooking.
5. Remove from the air fryer basket and transfer to a serving dish.

Nutritional Info (per serving):

- ✓ Calories – 198
- ✓ Fat – 2.4 g
- ✓ Fiber – 0.6 g
- ✓ Carbs – 15 g
- ✓ Protein – 28.9 g
- ✓ Sodium – 313 mg

Salmon Steak

Prep time: 5 min | **Cooking time**: 10 min | **Servings** 4

Salmon is one of the healthiest fish to include in your diet. It's rich in heart-friendly omega 3 fatty acids, and it's an excellent source of non-meat protein, selenium, potassium, and the B vitamins.

Cook it as a steak on the air fryer, and you'll preserve all the juices and flavors of this wonderful fish. In this recipe, paprika is added to the basic seasoning of salt and black pepper for that added kick.

Ingredients:

- 500 g salmon steak fillet
- ¼ tsp paprika
- ¼ tsp salt
- ⅛ tsp black pepper

Directions:

1. Preheat the air fryer at 265 F
2. Season the salmon steak with paprika, salt, and black pepper.
3. Place the salmon steak with the skin side down on the air fryer baking tray and cook for 10 minutes.
4. Transfer the cooked salmon steak and plate with your favorite sauce, and some optional side of asparagus.

Nutritional Info (per serving):

- ✓ Calories – 201
- ✓ Fat – 8.9 g
- ✓ Fiber – 0.1 g
- ✓ Carbs – 26 g
- ✓ Protein – 30.2 g
- ✓ Sodium – 216 mg

Fried Calamari Rings

Prep time: 15 min | **Cooking time**: 10-12 min | **Servings** 4

Squid (or more popularly known as calamari) contains phosphorous similar to shrimps and fish. To create a healthy balance of nutrients in your body, add several servings of seafood in your weekly meals on top of your usual fruit and vegetable servings.

This dish can be served as an appetizer or even a meal in itself with some side salad. Using the air fryer cuts back cooking time and ensures that you get that nice crunchy fried texture without the oil.

Ingredients:

- 400 g calamari, cut into ¼ inch rings
- 1 cup all-purpose flour
- ¼ tsp cayenne pepper
- ¼ tsp salt
- ⅛ tsp black pepper

Directions:

1. Preheat the air fryer to 375 F.
2. In a shallow pan, combine the all-purpose flour, cayenne pepper, salt, and black pepper.
3. Dredge the cleaned calamari rings in the flour mixture and make sure they are well coated.
4. Add the coated calamari rings in the air fryer basket and air fry for 10 minutes or until golden brown.
5. Transfer the air fried calamari rings to a serving dish and serve hot with optional air fried basil leaves as garnish.

Nutritional Info (per serving):

- ✓ Calories – 344
- ✓ Fat – 14.3 g
- ✓ Fiber – 0.9 g
- ✓ Carbs – 42 g
- ✓ Protein – 11.3 g
- ✓ Sodium – 148 mg

Trout Fillet

Prep time: 5 min | **Cooking time**: 10-12 min | **Servings** 4

Here's another healthy fish recipe to add to your meals. This recipe calls for trout which is another excellent source of omega-3 fatty acids, protein, potassium, phosphorous and the B-vitamin complex. Some experts even say it's one of the healthiest fish you can include in your diet.

As such, it's a good match to the air fryer as it cooks your fish without all that additional oil. To maximize the health benefits of trout, always use your air fryer. Never go back to traditional frying again.

Ingredients:

- 16 oz. trout fillets, boneless and skinless
- 1 lemon, juice
- 2 tbsp. olive oil
- ¼ tsp ground oregano
- ¼ tsp salt
- ⅛ tsp black pepper

Directions:

1. Preheat the air fryer to 390 F.
2. In a shallow baking dish, season the trout fillets in lemon juice, olive oil, ground oregano, salt, and black pepper.
3. Transfer to the air fryer basket and cook for 10-12 minutes, or until fully cooked.
4. Once cooked, place the air fried trout in a serving dish. Serve with optional carrots and peas.

Nutritional Info (per serving):

- ✓ Calories – 261
- ✓ Fat – 12.7 g
- ✓ Fiber – 0.5 g
- ✓ Carbs – 1.4 g
- ✓ Protein – 34.4 g
- ✓ Sodium – 83 mg

Tuna Steak

Prep time: 5 min | **Cooking time**: 8-10 min | **Servings** 4

Another omega-3 fatty fish to add to your diet is tuna. There are many varieties of tuna but go for the Ahi Tuna. Buy them fresh or get them frozen. Either way, you'll be getting a good dose of monounsaturated fats to help you maintain a healthy heart.

Cooking tuna steaks in an air fryer is absolutely easy. Just a quick seasoning, pop it in the air fryer, and you're done. If you want to dress up your tuna, add some side dishes like baked vegetables. It's a great one-dish meal even to help you lose pounds without sacrificing the nutrients.

Ingredients:

- 4 112-g ahi tuna steaks, raw, frozen or fresh
- 1 lemon, juice
- 2 tbsp. extra virgin olive oil
- ¼ tsp salt
- ¼ tsp black pepper

Directions:

1. Preheat the air fryer to 375 F.
2. Season the ahi tuna steaks with lemon juice salt, and black pepper.
3. Rub the tuna steaks with the extra virgin olive oil and make sure the fish is well coated in oil.
4. Place the seasoned tuna steak in the air fryer basket and cook for 8-10 minutes, flipping the steak halfway through the cooking for even cooking.
5. Transfer the cooked tuna steak on a serving platter, with optional roasted vegetables as side dish.

Nutritional Info (per serving):

- ✓ Calories – 185
- ✓ Fat – 8.0 g
- ✓ Fiber – 0.4 g
- ✓ Carbs – 1.4 g
- ✓ Protein – 26.2 g
- ✓ Sodium – 188 mg

Air Fried Dover Sole

Prep time: 5 min | **Cooking time**: 12 min | **Servings** 4

Dover Sole is a type of flatfish that is well suited for air frying. It has the B vitamins (B12, B1, B6, B2) plus folate, potassium, selenium, copper, zinc, iron, and calcium. Vitamin B12 is important to maintain healthy cells in the body, as it's the vitamin that produces DNA and RNA in the cells.

Here's a recipe for a classic grilled Dover Sole but adjusted for the air fryer technique. As always, simple is better to preserve the flavors of the fish.

Ingredients:

- 4 100-g Dover sole fillets, cleaned and skinned
- 1 lemon, juice and zest
- ¼ tsp nutmeg
- ¼ tsp salt
- ¼ cup parsley, chopped
- 1 tbsp. fresh dill

Directions:

1. Preheat the air fryer to 375 F.
2. In a baking pan, season the sole with lemon juice, lemon zest, chopped parsley, nutmeg, and salt.
3. Place the fish fillets in the air fryer and cook for 6 minutes on each side.
4. Once fully cooked, transfer the air fried fish fillets to a serving dish. Top with additional fresh chopped parsley, a wedge of lemon and some dill.

Nutritional Info (per serving):

- ✓ Calories – 89
- ✓ Fat – 1.2 g
- ✓ Fiber – 0.7 g
- ✓ Carbs – 2.2 g
- ✓ Protein – 17.5 g
- ✓ Sodium – 204 mg

Grilled Lemon Soy Halibut

Prep time: 5 min + 30 min marinating | **Cooking time**: 10-12 min | **Servings** 4

Grilling is proven to be one of the recommended cooking methods if you're striving to lose weight By grilling, you avoid the need to add a lot of ingredients, and thereby reduce the calories you consume.

Grilling in an air fryer is quick and easy. No need to prepare an elaborate grill setup. All you need is a little bit of time, a few ingredients and you'll have a healthy, grilled steak in a jiffy.

In this recipe, all you need are 4 ingredients and your trusty air fryer: halibut steaks and 3 readily available ingredients Halibut has a high dose of omega 3 fatty acids to help your cardiovascular health.

Ingredients:

- 400g halibut fillets
- 1 tbsp. soy sauce
- 1 lemon, juice
- ¼ tsp black pepper

Directions:

1. Preheat the air fryer to 390 F.
2. Marinate the halibut fillets in soy sauce, lemon juice, and black pepper.
3. Refrigerate and marinate for at least 30 minutes.
4. Transfer the marinated halibut steaks in a baking dish and place in the air fryer. Cook for 10-12 minutes.
5. Once cooked, place the halibut steaks on a serving dish, and serve with an optional steamed rice and a side salad.

Nutritional Info (per serving):

- ✓ Calories – 118
- ✓ Fat – 2.4 g
- ✓ Fiber – 0.4 g
- ✓ Carbs – 1.4 g
- ✓ Protein – 21.7 g
- ✓ Sodium – 283 mg

Fish Pie

Prep time: 5 min | **Cooking time**: 15-20 min | **Servings** 4

In this fish pie recipe, you can use any fish you like, but it's best to use a flaky type of fish such as salmon or cod. Here, we'll use salmon fillet (skinless) and cut them up into cubes.

Serve this dish in individual ramekins or bake in one large pie dish, depending on how you want to serve this fish pie.

Ingredients:

- 400 g salmon fillet, skinless, cut into cubes
- 1 tbsp. olive oil
- ¼ cup onions, chopped
- ½ cup tomatoes, chopped
- ¾ cup reduced fat milk
- ⅛ cup all-purpose flour
- ¼ cup parsley, chopped
- 1 cup mashed potatoes

Directions:

1. Preheat the air fryer to 350 F.
2. In a baking pan, place the chopped onions and tomatoes and drizzle the olive oil. Roast in the air fryer for 2 minutes.
3. Add the flour, milk, salmon cubes, and parsley and mix well together with the onion and tomatoes. Pre-cook for 3 minutes.
4. Place the salmon mixture into the ramekins and top with mashed potatoes.
5. Transfer the ramekins to the air fryer and continue cooking the fish pie for 10-15 minutes
6. Serve with an optional wedge of lemon.

Nutritional Info (per serving):

- ✓ Calories – 193
- ✓ Fat – 7.3 g
- ✓ Fiber – 0.7 g
- ✓ Carbs – 10.5 g
- ✓ Protein – 21.8 g
- ✓ Sodium – 321 mg

Baked Scallops

Prep time: 5 min | **Cooking time**: 4 min | **Servings** 4

We often hear about those perfectly seared scallops that are served in fancy restaurants. Well, if you want to cook scallops at home the easy well, look no further. The air fryer will help you cook those scallops the healthier and faster way.

Scallops are readily available frozen from supermarkets, so you can store them and plan ahead your meals whenever you feel like having some scallops.

Ingredients:

- 400g scallops, raw, frozen
- 2 tbsp. olive oil
- ¼ tsp black pepper

Directions:

1. Preheat the air fryer to 400 F.
2. Rub the scallops with olive oil, then season with black pepper.
3. Place the seasoned scallops in the air fryer and cook for 4 minutes.
4. Transfer the cooked scallops to a serving dish, or serve over a bowl of salad.

Nutritional Info (per serving):

- ✓ Calories – 150
- ✓ Fat – 7.5 g
- ✓ Fiber – 0.0 g
- ✓ Carbs – 2.8 g
- ✓ Protein – 16.9 g
- ✓ Sodium – 161 mg

Salmon in Teriyaki Steak Sauce

Prep time: 5 min | **Cooking time**: 10-12 min | **Servings** 4

This Asian-inspired recipe makes use of pink salmon fillet to ensure you're getting healthy fats into your diet. This savory dish is packed with rich flavors while maintaining a low-calorie count.

If you want to lose weight fast and still have energy from protein, consume a lot of fish and incorporate it into your diet. You'll watch those pounds just melt *away!*

Ingredients:

- 400 g pink salmon fillet
- ¼ tsp ginger powder
- 4 15-g serving teriyaki steak sauce
- ⅛ tsp garlic powder
- ⅛ tsp onion powder
- 1 tsp sesame oil

Directions:

1. Preheat the air fryer to 375 F.
2. In a baking dish, season the salmon fillets with ginger powder, garlic powder, onion powder, and sesame oil. Bake in the air fryer for 10 minutes.
3. Transfer the baked salmon fillet to a serving platter and drizzle on top with teriyaki sauce. Serve hot.

Nutritional Info (per serving):

- ✓ Calories – 151
- ✓ Fat – 4.7 g
- ✓ Fiber – 0.0 g
- ✓ Carbs – 4.2 g
- ✓ Protein – 20.4 g
- ✓ Sodium – 346 mg

Air Fryer Vegetarian Recipes

Air Fried Asparagus

Prep time: 15 min | **Cooking time**: 10-12 min | **Servings** 4

Who knows that even asparagus can be air fried? Yes, asparagus can be easily cooked using an air fryer in just a few minutes.

Aside from providing fiber, asparagus gives you a good amount of vitamin K, folate, chromium and also vitamins E and C. It also helps detoxify your body by breaking down carcinogens and free radicals. So load up on asparagus!

Ingredients:

- 4 cups asparagus
- 2 tbsp. olive oil
- ⅛ tsp salt
- ⅛ tsp black pepper
- ½ cup fresh strawberries halved

Directions:

1. Preheat the air fryer to 360 F.
2. Prepare the asparagus. Wash in running water, then remove the hard ends.
3. Cut all the spears in half, and toss in olive oil. Season with salt and black pepper.
4. Place the cut asparagus in the air fryer basket and air fry for 10 minutes.
5. Transfer the cooked asparagus to a serving platter. Add slices of fresh strawberries. Serve.

Nutritional Info (per serving):

- ✓ Calories – 93
- ✓ Fat – 7.2g
- ✓ Fiber – 3.2 g
- ✓ Carbs – 6.7 g
- ✓ Protein – 3.1 g
- ✓ Sodium – 77 mg

Tomato and Olive in Phyllo Pastry

Prep time: 10 min | **Cooking time**: 5-7 min | **Servings** 8

Working with phyllo pastry and combining it with vegetables is a great way to create healthy appetizers. In this recipe, we used vitamin-rich tomatoes and olives and added some dried herbs to tie the flavors together. Brushing the phyllo with olive oil will create that extra crunch as you bake this in your air fryer.

Use different types of tomatoes if you have access to heirloom or cherry tomatoes. A combination of tomato varieties will make this dish even more interesting, especially with the different colors.

Ingredients:

- 1 sheet phyllo pastry
- 1 large tomato, sliced thinly
- ½ cup olives, sliced
- ¼ tsp dried basil
- ⅛ tsp black pepper
- ¼ cup extra-virgin olive oil

Directions:

1. Preheat the air fryer to 400 F.
2. Cut the phyllo pastry sheets into squares that can fit your air fryer baking dish.
3. Brush the phyllo pastry squares with olive oil.
4. Place thin slices of tomatoes and sliced olives on top of the phyllo pastry squares. Sprinkle dried basil and black pepper.
5. Place the phyllo pastry squares in the air fryer and bake for 5 minutes or until the pastry has browned on the edges and has become crispy.
6. Transfer the baked phyllo pastry to a serving platter, and serve.

Nutritional Info (per serving):

- ✓ Calories – 151
- ✓ Fat – 7.9 g
- ✓ Fiber – 8.7 g
- ✓ Carbs – 22.9 g
- ✓ Protein – 3.8 g
- ✓ Sodium – 69 mg

Vegetarian Paella

Prep time: 10 min | **Cooking time**: 30 min | **Servings** 4

If you think paella can never be done in an air fryer, think again. Here's a recipe that allows you to make your own vegetarian paella with the convenience of an air fryer.

Paella is known for its numerous ingredients, but in this recipe, we trimmed it down to the bare essentials. You may use ready-packed paella seasonings, but this usually is loaded with sodium, so it's not really healthy. It's better to add these spices so you can control the salt better.

Ingredients:

- 150 g paella rice
- ½ cup green peas, raw
- 1 medium red bell pepper, sliced into strips
- 4 tbsp. sliced olives
- 1 large tomatoes, cut into wedges
- 1 cup vegetable stock + 1 cup water
- ½ tsp saffron
- ¼ tsp paprika
- ¼ tsp cayenne pepper
- ⅛ tsp black pepper
- 1 lemon, sliced into wedges

Directions:

1. Preheat the air fryer to 375F for about 5 minutes.
2. In a baking dish, combine the peas, bell pepper, olives, tomatoes, saffron, paprika, cayenne pepper, black pepper, and uncooked rice.
3. Add the vegetable stock and water to cover the rice mixture.
4. Cook in the air fryer for 30 minutes, checking every 10 minutes to stir the rice mixture.
5. Check the rice is fully cooked, or cook for additional 5 minutes if needed.
6. Depending on the rice used, you may add more water while cooking to prevent the rice from drying too much.
7. Once rice is fully cooked, carefully remove the baking dish from the air fryer.
8. Serve with lemon wedges.

Nutritional Info (per serving):

- ✓ Calories – 189
- ✓ Fat – 3.6 g
- ✓ Fiber – 2.5 g
- ✓ Carbs – 37.1 g
- ✓ Protein – 4.0 g
- ✓ Sodium – 327 mg

Stewed Tomato Soup

Prep time: 5 min | **Cooking time**: 5 min | **Servings** 2

Tomatoes are a must if you want to keep your body healthy. After all, tomatoes are rich in lycopene, a powerful antioxidant that helps fight diseases. It is one of the cancer-fighting foods that had been proven in several studies to slow down the growth cancel cells.

If you're trying to stay in shape or lose weight, soup is the way to go. It fills you up with roughage but not on the calories. With this tomato stew soup recipe, you'll not only lose the inches but gain tons of nutrients to keep you glowing.

Ingredients:

- 2 large tomatoes
- ¼ tsp dried ground oregano
- ¼ tsp dried ground cumin
- ¼ tsp dried basil
- ⅛ tsp salt
- ⅛ tsp black pepper
- 2 cups water

Directions:

1. Preheat the air fryer to 350 F.
2. In a baking dish, combine the tomatoes, dried oregano, ground cumin, dried basil, salt, black pepper, and water.
3. Cook in the air fryer for about 5 minutes, or until the tomatoes are soft and mashed.
4. Transfer to serving bowls, and serve hot.

Nutritional Info (per serving):

- ✓ Calories – 35
- ✓ Fat – 0.5 g
- ✓ Fiber – 2.4 g
- ✓ Carbs – 7.5 g
- ✓ Protein – 1.7 g
- ✓ Sodium – 157 mg

Roasted Curry Vegetables

Prep time: 15 min | **Cooking time**: 10-12 min | **Servings** 4

Depending on the season, you may find yourself having some sweet potatoes at home. Here's a recipe you can try so you can use those nutritious tubers. Using the air fryer, we'll roast them along with other vegetable and some seasonings.

This dish is rich in flavor and packed with strong flavors of the added spices, turmeric, and curry powder. It will go well with some plain white rice or brown rice if you like.

Ingredients:

- 2 cups sweet potatoes cubed
- 1 large zucchini, with skin, diced
- 1 cup mushrooms, raw pieces
- 2 tbsp. olive oil
- ½ tsp curry powder
- ½ tsp ground turmeric
- ⅛ tsp salt
- ⅛ tsp black pepper
- ½ cup water
- 1 tbsp. alfalfa sprouts

Directions:

1. Preheat the air fryer to 375 F.
2. In a baking dish, sweet potatoes, zucchini, button mushrooms, olive oil, curry powder, ground turmeric, salt, black pepper, and water. Mix well.
3. Cook in the air fryer for 30 minutes, checking every 10 minutes to mix. Add additional water if needed to prevent the vegetables from drying.
4. Once the vegetables are tender, transfer to a serving bowl.
5. Top with alfalfa sprouts. Serve.

Nutritional Info (per serving):

- ✓ Calories – 165
- ✓ Fat – 7.4 g
- ✓ Fiber – 4.2 g
- ✓ Carbs – 24.3 g
- ✓ Protein – 2.5 g
- ✓ Sodium – 90 mg

Vegetarian Sandwich

Prep time: 15 min | **Cooking time**: 5-6 min | **Servings** 4

This vegetarian patty recipe is loaded with protein and fiber, and low in calories. Using an air fryer, cooking burger patties is a walk in the park. Simply place them in the air fryer basket, and you're ready to fry – without the oil. Imagine all the calories and fats you cut down by simply switching to healthier burgers cooked the healthy way.

Adding mushrooms and beans into the patty will provide that deep, earthy flavor while the bell peppers will add a bit of crunch and mild pepper taste. The spinach is a bonus and makes this veggie burger super nutritious.

Ingredients:

- ½ cup cooked red kidney beans
- 1 small onion, minced
- 1 clove of garlic, minced
- ½ cup mushrooms, minced
- ¼ cup bell pepper, minced
- ¼ cup spinach, chopped
- 1 tbsp. mustard
- 1 tsp Worcestershire sauce
- ½ cup panko breadcrumbs

Directions:

1. Preheat the air fryer to 375 F.
2. In a mixing bowl, combine all the ingredients and blend well.
3. Form the vegetable mixture into 4 balls and flatten to make patties.
4. Place the patties in the air fryer and cook for 5-6 minutes, flipping the patty halfway in the cooking.
5. Transfer the cooked patties and assemble into a burger, or serve the patties as is.

Nutritional Info (per serving):

- ✓ Calories – 63
- ✓ Fat – 1.0 g
- ✓ Fiber – 2.8 g
- ✓ Carbs – 10.7 g
- ✓ Protein – 3.4 g
- ✓ Sodium – 21 mg

Vegetarian Noodle Soup

Prep time: 15 min | **Cooking time**: 10-12 min | **Servings** 4

Here's another soup recipe to fill you up using the air fryer, this time with some noodles. You may use any type of noodles, including the rice noodles that are used in this recipe. Adding noodles to this soup recipe will provide you enough carbohydrates to provide your body the energy you need, without too many calories.

To help increase your metabolism, a little bit of hot pepper sauce is added. You may omit the pepper sauce if you prefer the non-spicy version of this noodle soup.

Ingredients:

- 1 ½ cups rice noodles, cooked
- 2 cups water
- 1 small onion, chopped
- 1 clove garlic, minced
- ½ tsp ginger powder
- 1 medium carrot, sliced
- 1 medium radish, sliced
- 4-oz fish balls, cooked
- 1 tsp hot pepper sauce
- ⅛ tsp salt
- ⅛ tsp black pepper

Directions:

1. Preheat the air fryer to 375 F.
2. In a baking dish, combine all ingredients together.
3. Cook in the air fryer for 5 minutes or until the vegetables are tender.
4. Transfer the soup to serving bowls, and add additional seasoning as needed according to taste.

Nutritional Info (per serving):

- ✓ Calories – 138
- ✓ Fat – 3.7 g
- ✓ Fiber – 1.5 g
- ✓ Carbs – 21.5 g
- ✓ Protein – 4.1 g
- ✓ Sodium – 129 mg

Eggplant Parmigiana

Prep time: 10 min | **Cooking time**: 10-15 min | **Servings** 4

This Italian inspired dish is entirely meatless and features only eggplant, tomatoes, some dried herbs for seasoning, and vegetarian cheese.

Perfect as a vegetable entrée, this recipe can also be prepared for small potluck parties or even cut up into small pieces as appetizers.

Ingredients:

- 2 large eggplant, thinly sliced lengthwise
- 2 oz. vegetarian parmesan cheese
- 1 cup fresh tomatoes, chopped
- 1 tbsp. olive oil
- ¼ tsp dried basil
- ⅛ tsp salt
- ⅛ tsp black pepper

Directions:

1. Preheat the air fryer to 350 F.
2. In a baking dish, placed a layer of chopped tomatoes. Drizzle with olive oil, then season with salt, and black pepper.
3. Lay the eggplant slices over the tomatoes, then top with shredded vegetarian cheese and dried basil.
4. Cook in the air fryer for 10-15 minutes or until the cheese is golden brown.
5. Remove the baking dish from the air fryer and serve.

Nutritional Info (per serving):

- ✓ Calories – 162
- ✓ Fat – 7.6 g
- ✓ Fiber – 10.3 g
- ✓ Carbs – 18.0 g
- ✓ Protein – 8.1 g
- ✓ Sodium – 211 mg

Tofu with Broccoli

Prep time: 10 min | **Cooking time**: 5-10 min | **Servings** 4

A popular combination, tofu, and broccoli are great ingredients to cook in an air fryer because of how they turn brown to the heat. In effect, they can become crunchy depending on how long you cook them in the air fryer.

This recipe is also great as a spicy dish, so if you can take the heat, garnish with some slices pepper for that extra kick of flavor.

Ingredients:

- ½ block firm tofu, cut into squares
- 2 cups broccoli florets
- 2 tbsp. olive oil
- ⅛ tsp salt
- ⅛ tsp black pepper
- 1 tsp (approx. 10g) sliced chili peppers (optional)

Directions:

1. Preheat the air fryer to 375 F.
2. In a baking dish, combine the tofu squares, broccoli florets, olive oil, salt, and black pepper. Mix well to blend all ingredients together.
3. Cook in the air fryer for 5-10 minutes or until the tofu turns golden brown.
4. Transfer the cooked broccoli and tofu to a serving platter.
5. Top with optional slices of chili pepper.

Nutritional Info (per serving):

- ✓ Calories – 91
- ✓ Fat – 8.0 g
- ✓ Fiber – 1.5 g
- ✓ Carbs – 3.7 g
- ✓ Protein – 2.9 g
- ✓ Sodium – 90 mg

Oyster Mushrooms

Prep time: 15 min | **Cooking time**: 10-12 min | **Servings** 4

This mushroom recipe is great as an appetizer or a side dish. Use button mushrooms as they have that nice shape for serving as appetizers. If you prefer, you may also serve button mushrooms whole instead of halved.

Don't underestimate these mushrooms as they are full of nutrients. Compared to oyster or shiitake mushrooms, button mushrooms a.k.a. Champignons have more selenium, protein, copper as well as potassium.

Ingredients:

- 2 cups sliced button mushrooms
- 1 tbsp. olive oil
- ⅛ tsp black pepper
- ¼ cup fresh parsley, chopped
- 1 tbsp. oyster sauce

Directions:

1. Preheat the air fryer to 350 F.
2. In a mixing bowl, toss the mushrooms in olive oil and season with black pepper.
3. Cook the mushrooms in the air fryer and air fry for 10 minutes or until the mushrooms have browned.
4. Transfer the cooked mushrooms to a serving platter.
5. Add the fresh parsley on top of the mushrooms, then drizzle with oyster sauce according to taste.

Nutritional Info (per serving):

- ✓ Calories – 45
- ✓ Fat – 3.5 g
- ✓ Fiber – 1.2 g
- ✓ Carbs – 2.6 g
- ✓ Protein – 0.7 g
- ✓ Sodium – 245 mg

Veggie Spring Rolls

Prep time: 15 min | **Cooking time**: 10 min | **Servings** 4

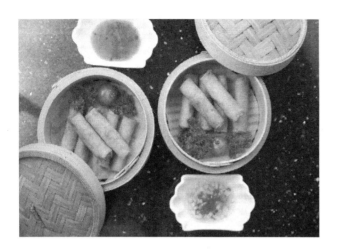

Veggie spring rolls are ideal for appetizers, snacks or even as picnic food. Typically these little pockets of goodness are deep fried in a large pan of hot oil. But using your air fryer, you'll get the same crispness without all that oil.

The trio of vegetables used in this recipe (bean sprouts, French beans, and carrots) make this dish rich in fiber which is good for your digestion. You'll love the bean sprouts for they add that nutty flavor and very low in calories.

Ingredients:

- 4 pcs spring roll wrapper
- 1 cup bean sprouts, raw
- ½ cup shredded French beans, raw
- ½ cup grated carrots, raw
- 1 tsp pure sesame oil
- ¼ tsp onion powder
- ¼ tsp garlic powder
- ⅛ tsp salt
- ⅛ tsp black pepper

Directions:

1. Preheat the air fryer to 400 F.
2. In a mixing bowl, mix together all the vegetables and season with sesame oil, onion powder, garlic powder, salt, and black pepper.
3. Place in the air fryer and cook for 5 minutes or until the vegetables are cooked.
4. Transfer the cooked vegetables into a container and let cool for 2 minutes.
5. Prepare the wrap the cooked vegetables in spring roll wrappers. Scoop about 1 to 2 tbsp. of filling into the spring roll wrapper. Moisten the edges with water to seal.
6. Place the spring rolls into the air fryers basket and cook for 5 minutes or until the wrapper has turned golden brown.
7. Transfer the air fried spring rolls to a serving platter of your choice.

Nutritional Info (per serving):

- ✓ Calories – 177
- ✓ Fat – 2.9 g
- ✓ Fiber – 6.7 g
- ✓ Carbs – 30.9 g
- ✓ Protein – 6.3 g
- ✓ Sodium – 259 mg

Veggie Balls

Prep time: 15 min | **Cooking time**: 10 min | **Servings** 4

If you want the flavor and nutrients of vegetables without any wrapping, then veggie balls are for you. These 2-bite savory snacks go well with some creamy low-fat Greek yogurt dip or some sweet chili sauce. To simplify, you can just eat them on their own.

These veggie balls are low in fat and zero in cholesterol while providing your body adequate dietary fiber, vitamin D, and iron.

Ingredients:

- 1 cup lentils, cooked
- 1 cup mushroom, raw pieces
- ½ cup celery stalks and leaves, chopped
- ½ cup carrot, grated
- 1 tbsp. olive oil
- ½ tsp onion powder
- ½ tsp garlic powder
- ⅛ tsp salt
- ⅛ tsp black pepper
- ¾ cup panko breadcrumbs

Directions:

1. Preheat the air fryer to 350 F.
2. In a mixing bowl, combine the lentils, mushroom, celery, and carrots and mix thoroughly. Season with olive oil, onion powder, garlic powder, salt, and black pepper.
3. Add the breadcrumbs to the mixture and mix well.
4. Form the mixture into balls about 1-1/2 inch in diameter.
5. Transfer the veggie balls into the air fryer basket and air fry for 5-10 minutes or until the balls are golden brown.
6. Once cooked, place the veggie balls on a serving platter and serve with an optional Greek yogurt dip or some sweet chili sauce.

Nutritional Info (per serving):

- ✓ Calories – 115
- ✓ Fat – 3.8 g
- ✓ Fiber – 4.8 g
- ✓ Carbs – 15.6 g
- ✓ Protein – 5.7 g
- ✓ Sodium – 101 mg

Healthy Vegetarian Casserole

Prep time: 10 min | **Cooking time**: 5-10 min | **Servings** 4

Casseroles are ideal for a small party or on a potluck table.

Ingredients:

- 1 large zucchini, sliced 1-cm. thick
- 2 large tomato, sliced 1-cm. thick
- 1 medium onion, diced
- ¼ cup fresh parsley, chopped
- 2 oz vegetarian parmesan
- 1 tbsp olive oil
- ⅛ tsp salt
- ⅛ tsp black pepper

Directions:

1. Preheat the air fryer to 390 F.
2. In a baking dish, layer the slices of zucchini and tomatoes. Drizzle with olive oil, then season with salt and black pepper.
3. Top the vegetables with vegetarian parmesan.
4. Place the dish in the air fryer and bake for 5-10 minutes or until the parmesan cheese is golden brown.
5. Remove the dish from the air fryer and let it cool for 1-2 minutes.
6. Top with fresh parsley. Serve.

Nutritional Info (per serving):

- ✓ Calories – 127
- ✓ Fat – 7.4 g
- ✓ Fiber – 2.7 g
- ✓ Carbs – 9.1 g
- ✓ Protein – 7.2 g
- ✓ Sodium – 219 mg

Vegetable Ragout

Prep time: 15 min | **Cooking time**: 10-12 min | **Servings** 4

Don't be confused between a ragu and a ragout. While ragu is a type of Italian pasta sauce, a ragout is a slow-cooked French-style stew. In this recipe, we're doing an air fry version of a vegetable ragout.

This recipe calls for a medley of mushrooms, tomatoes, zucchini, and onions. The onions will help create that brown caramelized color once the vegetables are roasted in the air fryer.

Ingredients:

- 1 large zucchini, sliced 1-cm thick
- 1 cup button mushrooms, quartered
- 2 large tomato, quartered
- 2 large onion, diced
- 1 tbsp. olive oil
- ⅛ tsp salt
- ⅛ tsp black pepper

Directions:

1. Preheat the air fryer to 350 F.
2. In a baking pan, combine all the cut vegetables and season with olive oil, salt, and black pepper.
3. Roast in the air fryer for 10-12 minutes or until the onions become fully caramelized. Check halfway through the cooking to mix the vegetables for even cooking.
4. Transfer the cooked vegetables to a serving platter. Serve alongside an optional starch of your choice.

Nutritional Info (per serving):

- ✓ Calories – 97
- ✓ Fat – 4.0 g
- ✓ Fiber – 4.0 g
- ✓ Carbs – 14.5 g
- ✓ Protein – 3.7 g
- ✓ Sodium – 91 mg

Vegetarian Quesadilla

Prep time: 10 min | **Cooking time**: 5-8 min | **Servings** 4

Here's another vegetarian dish that spells "p-a-r-t-y"! Quesadillas conjure images of festivities and merry-making. With your air fryer, you can easily create this dish with just a few ingredients.

This recipe is good as an appetizer. You can slice the quesadillas into wedges and can be eaten as finger food.

Ingredients:

- 2 pcs. whole wheat flour tortilla
- 1 cup vegan mozzarella style shreds
- ½ cup sweet red pepper, diced
- ½ cup tomatoes, diced
- ⅛ tsp black pepper

Directions:

1. Preheat the air fryer to 375 F.
2. Spread the diced sweet red pepper and tomatoes on half of the flour tortilla.
3. Top with vegan mozzarella style shreds.
4. Fold the flour tortilla, so you form a half moon shape. Do the same for the other flour tortilla.
5. Place the quesadillas in the air fryer and bake for 5-8 minutes or until they start to brown.
6. Transfer the cooked quesadillas to a serving dish. Slice into wedges.
7. Serve with an optional salsa or guacamole dip.

Nutritional Info (per serving):

- ✓ Calories – 101
- ✓ Fat – 4.1 g
- ✓ Fiber – 2.0 g
- ✓ Carbs – 13.8 g
- ✓ Protein – 2.1 g
- ✓ Sodium – 129 mg

Baked Stuffed Mushrooms

Prep time: 15 min | **Cooking time**: 15 min | **Servings** 8

Mushrooms are so versatile you can even stuff them! In this recipe, you'll learn how to prepare baked stuffed mushrooms using your air fryer. Use regular button mushrooms as they are perfect for stuffing compared to other types of mushrooms. You can also use Cremini mushrooms.

Plan ahead when you prepare this dish, especially when you're making plenty of servings. It's best when you serve the mushrooms right after cooking.

Ingredients:

- 24 pieces button mushrooms, stems separated from the caps and minced
- 1 medium onion, minced
- 1 clove of garlic, minced
- ¼ cup walnuts, chopped
- ½ cup breadcrumbs
- 2 oz. vegetarian parmesan
- 2 tbsp. olive oil
- ⅛ tsp salt
- ⅛ tsp black pepper

Directions:

1. Preheat the air fryer to 375 F.
2. Prepare the filling. In a baking dish, combine the mushroom stems with all the ingredients. Mix well.
3. Place in the air fryer and cook for 8-10 minutes.
4. Remove the cooked filling from the air fryer and prepare to stuff them into the mushroom caps.
5. Scoop about a teaspoon or two into each mushroom, depending on the size of your button mushrooms.
6. Bake the stuffed mushroom in the air fryer for 5 minutes.
7. Transfer to a serving platter and garnish with optional parsley sprigs. Serve immediately.

Nutritional Info (per serving):

- ✓ Calories – 136
- ✓ Fat – 5.1 g
- ✓ Fiber – 6.8 g
- ✓ Carbs – 12.4 g
- ✓ Protein – 9.8 g
- ✓ Sodium – 156 mg

Air Fried Chickpeas

Prep time: 5 min | **Cooking time**: 20 min | **Servings** 8

Air fried chickpeas are the ultimate snack that's rich in nutrients and rich in fun. Using an air fryer, these chickpeas will turn crunchy and crispy. You'll never stop munching this!

Don't worry as chickpeas are good sources of protein and fiber. And since this is fried in the hot air instead of oil, you'll assure you're getting none of those bad fats.

Ingredients:

- 200g dry chickpeas, cooked
- 1 tbsp. olive oil
- ¼ tsp onion powder
- ¼ tsp garlic powder
- ¼ tsp ground cumin
- ⅛ tsp salt
- ⅛ tsp black pepper

Directions:

1. Preheat the air fryer to 350 F.
2. In a mixing bowl, combine cooked chickpeas with olive oil, onion powder, garlic powder, ground cumin, salt, and black pepper. Toss until well blended.
3. Place in the air fryer and cook for 15 minutes.
4. Open the air fryer basket and mix the chickpeas. Cook for additional 5 minutes or until chickpeas has turned brown.
5. Transfer to a serving bowl and eat as a snack.

Nutritional Info (per serving):

- ✓ Calories – 107
- ✓ Fat – 3.3 g
- ✓ Fiber – 4.4 g
- ✓ Carbs – 15.4 g
- ✓ Protein – 4.9 g
- ✓ Sodium – 41 mg

Air Fryer Baking & Desserts Recipes

Carrot Cake

Prep time: 10 min | **Cooking time**: 10 min | **Servings** 8

Carrot cake has a very light and delicate taste. It's useful and low-calorie!

Ingredients:

- 1 cup self-rising flour
- 1 cup brown sugar
- ½ tsp cinnamon powder
- 1 large carrot, peeled and shredded
- ½ tsp nutmeg
- 1 large egg
- ¼ cup olive oil
- 1 tbsp. reduced fat milk

Directions:

1. Preheat the air fryer to 350 F.
2. In a mixing bowl, combine the flour, cinnamon powder, nutmeg, carrots, and sugar. Blend well with totally mixed.
3. Add the egg, olive oil, and milk into the flour mixture and continue mixing.
4. Pour the cake batter into a greased baking pan and cook for 10-12 minutes or until cooked.
5. You may add an optional frosting by combining ¼ cup icing sugar with 1 tbsp melted butter and juice from 1 orange.
6. Transfer carrot cake to a serving platter and serve.

Nutritional Info (per serving):

- ✓ Calories – 185
- ✓ Fat – 7.0 g
- ✓ Fiber – 1.1 g
- ✓ Carbs – 30.1 g
- ✓ Protein – 1.0 g
- ✓ Sodium – 24 mg

Donut recipe

Prep time: 10 min | **Cooking time**: 15 min | **Servings** 4

However you want to spell it – doughnuts or donuts – this is one sweet stuff you can try creating in your air fryer. Donuts are typically deep fried in hot oil, but with an air fryer, you can skill the hot and use hot air to cook them.

In this recipe, we'll be baking donuts without the hole. Of course, if you like it with holes, go ahead the make them! Either way, your donuts will turn out lovely. Top with your favorite nuts or glaze, or go simple with a light dusting of confectioners' sugar.

Ingredients:

- 2 cups self-rising flour
- ½ cup granulated sugar
- ½ cup reduced fat milk
- 1 tsp low-sodium baking powder
- ½ tsp cinnamon powder
- 2 tbsp. olive oil
- 1 medium egg
- 1 tsp vanilla extract

Directions:

1. Preheat the air fryer to 390 F.
2. In a mixing bowl, sift together the flour, sugar, baking powder, cinnamon powder.
3. In another bowl, combine the milk, olive oil, egg, and vanilla extract until well blended.
4. Slowly add the liquid mixture to the dry mixture and gently mix until you form a dough.
5. On a floured surface, flatten the dough (about 1 inch thick) and cut into circles using a cookie cutter.
6. Add the circular doughs into the air fryer and bake for 15 minutes or until fully cooked.
7. Take the baked donuts out of the air fryer and let cool for 1-2 minutes before dusting with confectioner sugar
8. Place on a serving platter and serve.

Nutritional Info (per serving):

- ✓ Calories – 246
- ✓ Fat – 8.7 g
- ✓ Fiber – 3.5 g
- ✓ Carbs – 32.7 g
- ✓ Protein – 2.4 g
- ✓ Sodium – 31 mg

Orange Cupcakes

Prep time: 10 min | **Cooking time**: 15 min | **Servings** 12

For this cupcake recipe, the featured flavor is that of orange, a refreshing citrus fruit that boasts of vitamin C to help increase your body's resistance to infections. We'll use both the juice and zest of the orange to achieve that full flavor. Just one fruit provides you 130% of your daily vitamin C needs. Aside from vitamin C, oranges are also a good source of vitamin A for better eye health.

Oranges also help in brain development since they contain folic acid. No wonder it's highly recommended, especially for child-bearing women to help the baby's neurological health.

Ingredients:

- ¼ cup butter softened
- 1 cup low-fat Greek yogurt
- 1 cup granulated sugar
- 2 eggs
- 1 tbsp. orange zest
- 1 orange, juice
- 1 ½ cup all-purpose flour
- 1 ½ tsp low-sodium baking powder
- ¼ tsp salt

Directions:

1. Preheat the air fryer to 350 F.
2. In a mixing bowl, sift together the flour, baking powder
3. In a mixing bowl, combine butter and yogurt, sugar, eggs, orange zest, and juice.
4. Add the liquid mixture to the dry mixture and mix well.
5. Spoon the batter into ramekins lined with cupcake liners.
6. Place the ramekins in the air fryer and bake for 13-15 minutes or until fully baked.
7. Remove the baked cupcakes from the air fryer and let cool for 1-2 minutes before lightly dusting with powdered sugar.

Nutritional Info (per serving):

- ✓ Calories – 139
- ✓ Fat – 4.9 g
- ✓ Fiber – 0.2 g
- ✓ Carbs – 22.8 g
- ✓ Protein – 2.1 g
- ✓ Sodium – 80 mg

Blueberry Muffins

Prep time: 10 min | **Cooking time**: 10-12 min | **Servings** 12

Are you looking for the fountain of youth? It's time to load up with blueberries! These dark purple jewels have antioxidants that fight aging. In fact, it's one of the highest antioxidant foods you can find.

They are also rich in proanthocyanin which helps fight cancer. If you want to lose weight or keep your skin young looking, the proanthocyanin will also do that for you. With its soluble and insoluble fiber, these fruits help regulate your gut health as well.

Ready to enjoy these health benefits in the form of delicious muffins? Bake on!

Ingredients:

- 1 ½ cup cake flour
- ½ cup granulated sugar
- 2 tsp baking powder
- ½ tsp salt
- ¼ cup olive oil
- 1 egg
- 1 cup low-fat Greek yogurt
- 1 cup blueberries, fresh

Directions:

1. Preheat the air fryer to 390 F.
2. In a mixing bowl, sift together the cake flour, granulated sugar, baking powder, and salt.
3. In another bowl, combine the wet ingredients: olive oil, egg, and yogurt.
4. Add the wet to the dry ingredients gently until well mixed.
5. Fold in the blueberries gently to avoid bursting the berries.
6. Spoon the batter into ramekins lined with muffin liner.
7. Place the ramekins in the air fryer and bake for 10-12 minutes or until fully baked.
8. Take the baked out of the air fryer and let cool for 1-2 minutes.
9. Transfer to a serving platter and serve.

Nutritional Info (per serving):

- ✓ Calories – 105
- ✓ Fat – 4.9 g
- ✓ Fiber – 0.4 g
- ✓ Carbs – 14.7 g
- ✓ Protein – 1.6 g
- ✓ Sodium – 121 mg

Chocolate Brownie

Prep time: 10 min | **Cooking time**: 20 min | **Servings** 8

Chocolate Brownie is the top of gastronomic pleasure at the relative simplicity of cooking.

Ingredients:

- ¾ cup unsweetened cocoa powder
- ½ cup self-rising flour
- 1 egg
- 1 cup sugar
- ¼ tsp salt
- ½ cup olive oil
- 1 tsp vanilla
- ½ cup walnuts

Directions:

1. Preheat the air fryer to 390 F.
2. In a mixing bowl, combine egg, sugar, olive oil, and vanilla. Blend well.
3. In another mixing bowl, sift together the flour, cocoa powder, and salt.
4. Gradually add the dry ingredients to the wet ingredients and mix well. Fold in the walnuts.
5. Prepare a baking pan that can fit your air fryer. Line it with parchment paper, then pour the batter into the baking pan.
6. Place inside the air fryer basket and bake for 20 minutes.
7. Once baked, take the brownie out of the air fryer and let cool for 1-2 minutes.
8. Cut into squares, then serve.

Nutritional Info (per serving):

- ✓ Calories – 255
- ✓ Fat – 15.9 g
- ✓ Fiber – 4.2 g
- ✓ Carbs – 32.1 g
- ✓ Protein – 3.1 g
- ✓ Sodium – 29 mg

Scones

Prep time: 15 min | **Cooking time**: 10 min | **Servings** 4

Scones are very British, but with an air fryer, practically anyone can master this dish in no time. Serve this for an afternoon tea, or perhaps for your weekend breakfast.

This recipe is adjusted for the air fryer, and you may add in some variations to the recipe. For instance, you may add some dried fruits like cranberries.

Ingredients:

- 2 cups self-rising flour
- 4 tsp unsalted butter
- 1 cup reduced fat milk
- ¼ tsp salt
- 1 tsp honey

Directions:

1. Preheat the air fryer to 400 F.
2. In a mixing bowl, combine flour and salt.
3. Add the butter and crumble it into the flour mixture.
4. Add the milk and honey and blend into the flour mixture until you form a dough.
5. Knead the dough lightly on a floured surface and spread it to about ½ inch thick.
6. Using a cookie cutter, cut the flattened dough into rounds.
7. Place all the cut round dough on a greased baking tray and place inside the air fryer. Bake for 10 minutes or until the scones are golden brown.
8. Transfer baked scones to a serving dish, and serve with optional clotted cream or jam.

Nutritional Info (per serving):

- ✓ Calories – 119
- ✓ Fat – 5.0 g
- ✓ Fiber – 3.5 g
- ✓ Carbs – 12.4 g
- ✓ Protein – 2.1 g
- ✓ Sodium – 177 mg

Oatmeal Cookies

Prep time: 10 min | **Cooking time**: 8 min | **Servings** 8

Oatmeal raisin cookie is one of the life's simple indulgences. It's a sweet treat yet it's healthy at the same time with fiber that the oats provide.

In this recipe, we'll add some raisins for additional fiber as well as B vitamins, iron and potassium. They're also a good source of carbohydrates for energy so feel free to munch on these as power snacks.

If you're keeping an eye on your cholesterol count, the oats in these cookies will help to lower it. Maintaining a diet rich in oats will greatly reduce the risk of coronary heart diseases as well as colorectal cancer.

Ingredients:

- ½ cup brown sugar, packed
- ⅓ cup unsalted butter, softened
- 1 egg, large
- 1 cup oats, quick cooking
- ½ cup all-purpose flour
- ½ tsp cinnamon powder
- ½ tsp baking soda
- ⅛ tsp salt
- ½ cup raisins, seedless

Directions:

1. Preheat the air fryer to 350 F.
2. In a mixing bowl, cream the brown sugar and butter until well blended.
3. Add the egg and mix until creamy.
4. Add the dry ingredients to the mixture: oats, flour, cinnamon powder, baking soda, and salt.
5. Finally, add the raisins. Mix everything together.
6. On a greased baking dish, scoop the batter into cookie balls about 1 tablespoon per cookie. Flatten the balls a little, and leave a distance of about 1-2 inches in between.
7. Bake in the air fryer for 8 minutes.
8. Remove from the air fryer and let cool for 1-2 minutes.
9. Serve or store in an airtight cookie jar.

Nutritional Info (per serving):

- ✓ Calories – 165
- ✓ Fat – 8.5 g
- ✓ Fiber – 0.7 g
- ✓ Carbs – 22.1 g
- ✓ Protein – 1.7 g
- ✓ Sodium – 125 mg

Cornbread Muffin

Prep time: 10 min | **Cooking time**: 10-12 min | **Servings** 8

This cornbread muffin recipe is based on the classic Southern favorite but with a healthier twist. Cornmeal is an important ingredient for those who cannot take gluten as it's one of the flours that don't have gluten in it. While this recipe is not entirely gluten-free, you can still adjust it to make it such if you prefer.

Simply replace with all-purpose flour with a gluten-free flour blend, and you're good to go.

Ingredients:

- ¾ cup cornmeal, whole-grain yellow
- 1 cup all-purpose flour
- 1 tsp low sodium baking powder
- ¼ tsp salt
- ¼ cup brown sugar, packed
- 1 cup reduced fat milk
- 1 medium egg
- ¼ cup olive oil

Directions:

1. Preheat the air fryer to 400 F.
2. In a mixing bowl, combine all dry ingredients: cornmeal, flour, baking powder, salt and brown sugar.
3. Into the dry ingredients, add the milk, egg and olive oil. Mix until you get a smooth batter.
4. Pour the batter into ramekins and bake in the air fryer for 10-12 minutes or until the crust is golden brown.
5. Transfer the baked cornmeal muffins to a serving platter and serve.

Nutritional Info (per serving):

- ✓ Calories – 161
- ✓ Fat – 7.9 g
- ✓ Fiber – 1.0 g
- ✓ Carbs – 21.1 g
- ✓ Protein – 3.0 g
- ✓ Sodium – 104 mg

The Healthy Pound Cake

Prep time: 10 min | **Cooking time**: 20-25 min | **Servings** 8

Pound cakes are notorious for being unhealthy especially with all the eggs added. This recipe, however, makes some adjustments to the classic pound cake recipe. It adds healthier ingredients such as olive and yogurt to replace the usual butter.

Moreover, it uses white whole-wheat flour instead of the more commonly used all-purpose flour. If you have white whole-wheat flour, use it. If not, all-purpose flour will do.

Ingredients:

- ¼ cup olive oil
- ¼ cup low-fat Greek yogurt
- ½ cup sugar
- 1 cups white whole-wheat flour
- 1 large egg
- 2 large egg whites
- 1 tsp pure vanilla extract
- ¼ tsp salt

Directions:

1. Preheat the air fryer to 350 F.
2. Combine the olive oil, yogurt, and sugar together and mix well.
3. Add the eggs and egg white, vanilla, and salt to yogurt mixture and whisk until smooth.
4. Gradually add the flour until well combined with the rest of the ingredients.
5. Pour the batter into a greased baking pan, and bake in the air fryer for 20-25 minutes depending on the size of the baking pan. Check by inserting a toothpick into the cake. If it comes out clean, it's cooked.
6. Take out the baking pan and let cool for 1-2 minutes before removing the cake from the pan.
7. Slice and place on a serving platter. Serve.

Nutritional Info (per serving):

- ✓ Calories – 131
- ✓ Fat – 7.1 g
- ✓ Fiber – 0.4 g
- ✓ Carbs – 15.7 g
- ✓ Protein – 2.5 g
- ✓ Sodium – 97 mg

Vanilla Tart

Prep time: 10 min | **Cooking time**: 10-13 min | **Servings** 4

This recipe for pudding tart is adjusted to accommodate a few healthier substitutions. For instance, instead of using whole milk for the pudding, try to use reduced-fat milk. Similarly, you can replace butter with other forms of healthier fats such as olive oil.

The flavor profile of this pudding tart is on vanilla. While others would probably squeeze a dollop of whipped cream on top, we highly recommend you skip it and just use fresh fruits on top to liven up the tarts.

Ingredients:

- 4 pcs tart shells, frozen
- 1 tbsp. cornstarch
- ⅛ tsp salt
- 1 cup reduced fat milk
- 1 large egg yolk
- ½ cup sugar
- ¼ cup water
- 1 tbsp. olive oil
- ½ tsp vanilla extract

Directions:

1. Preheat the air fryer to 375 F for about 5 minutes.
2. In a baking dish, combine the cornstarch, salt, and milk and whisk until well blended.
3. Add in the egg yolk and keep whisking.
4. Add the sugar, water, olive oil, and vanilla extract to the mixture. Place inside the air fryer and cook the pudding for 5 minutes.
5. Check the pudding, stir to smooth out any lumps that may have formed. Cook for additional 2-3 minutes or until pudding thickens.
6. Remove the thicken pudding from the air fryer and transfer to the tart shells.
7. Place the filled tart shells in the air fryer and cook for 5 minutes or until the tart shells have browned on the edges.
8. Transfer the baked pudding tarts to a serving platter and serve.

Nutritional Info (per serving):

- ✓ Calories – 267
- ✓ Fat – 10.4 g
- ✓ Fiber – 0.0 g
- ✓ Carbs – 41.0 g
- ✓ Protein – 3.7 g
- ✓ Sodium – 127 mg

New York Cheesecake

Prep time: 15 min | **Cooking time**: 20 min | **Servings** 8

This low-fat cheesecake recipe makes use of fat-free cream cheese and fat-free sour cream. If you can find those ingredients, then it would make a lot of difference in the fat content. However, if in case you don't have them on hand, you can still use regular cream cheese and sour cream for this recipe.

This is a basic recipe so you can still add your favorite toppings, or serve it alongside some fruits.

Ingredients:

For the crust:
- ½ cup honey graham cracker crumbs
- 1 tbsp. butter

For the filling:
- 1 cup fat-free cream cheese
- ¼ cup sugar
- ½ cup fat-free sour cream
- 2 eggs

Directions:

1. Preheat the air fryer to 350 F.
2. Prepare the crust by combining the graham crumbs and butter. Press the crust mixture into the bottom of a pan to form the base of the cheesecake. Bake for 4 minutes, then allow for cooling for 5 minutes.
3. Meanwhile, prepare the cheesecake filling. Combine sugar, the cream cheese, sour cream, and eggs and blend together.
4. Pour the cheesecake filling into the crust and bake for 15 minutes at 310 F.
5. Once baked, remove from the air fryer. Chill before serving.

Nutritional Info (per serving):

- ✓ Calories – 186
- ✓ Fat – 3.2 g
- ✓ Fiber – 0.1 g
- ✓ Carbs – 31.8 g
- ✓ Protein – 7.8 g
- ✓ Sodium – 227 mg

Conclusion

With a revolutionary kitchen appliance like the air fryer, cooking easy, healthy and delicious meals at home has become more practical. Not only will you be saving time but more importantly, you'll be cutting back on oil in your food.

Just remember that a little goes a long way. Once you get in the habit of air frying your foods, you'll never return to traditional pan or deep frying ever again.

Your body will thank you for cooking food the best way possible.

We hope with this cookbook you were able to explore further the power of the air fryer in preparing a variety of dishes. You now have discovered a whole new world of cooking via rapidly circulating hot air instead of hot oil.

The air fryer is simply the perfect companion for any home cook who wants to create dishes that are nutritious and quick to prepare.

Now go ahead and enjoy cooking happy air frying!

Made in the USA
Lexington, KY
08 March 2018